Jim, Barry and Michael have produced a ⸺ relevant read on leadership and engagement. Reassuringly, they demonstrate that great leadership is grounded in common sense and humanity. That is consistent with our experience at Virgin. The book benefits enormously from a wealth of real-world examples. It is notable that many of the leaders whose experience is referred to are not CEOs, but rather people at all levels of a variety of different organisations who have faced the challenges inherent in successfully leading people. It is axiomatic that successful leadership results in high employee engagement. In purely commercial terms, engagement creates a sustainable competitive advantage. It also acknowledges the broader role of business in the community to develop people to their fullest potential. The authors have produced a work in an Australasian context that identifies universal rules that will be of value to all people managers who want to take on new challenges or refresh their approach to achieve more.

—**Josh Bayliss, CEO, Virgin Group (Worldwide)**

I have been using The Five Practices framework to develop my executive and managerial students' leadership skills, and in the past I had to make the necessary adjustments to connect those practices to the distinctive elements of leadership in the Australasian region. Happily, this new book makes those adjustments for me, offering many useful examples that connect directly to my students' experience. The framework is now even more relevant and appropriate for Australasian students and practitioners.

—**Arran Caza, Associate Professor of Management,**
Griffith Business School

I am delighted to see The Five Practices of Exemplary Leadership brought to life and embedded in our historically and geographically distinctive Australasian leadership context. This classic and globally practised approach to leadership has stood the test of time in the way that many others have not. The exemplary leaders that are liberally featured in this book provide compelling evidence of the power of this framework as it has been applied to a wide range of organisations within Australia and New Zealand. This book should become a compulsory mainstay of the leadership libraries of both emerging and established leaders from all sectors of the economy.

— **Professor Brad Jackson, Head of School of Government, Victoria University of Wellington, New Zealand**

The authors effectively demonstrate that great leaders can be made, not born, if only they take their people on the journey with them. These five principles are compulsory reading for all prospective leaders and for those seeking more sustainable success.

— **Mandy Johnson, author of *Family Village Tribe* and *Winning the War for Talent***

What an absolute delight it is to read this new take on the classic *The Leadership Challenge*. There is no doubt that when it comes to leadership, culture really matters, and Jim, Barry and Michael have written the definitive guide for those in Australia and New Zealand. With fresh local examples and case studies, this is a must-read book.

— **Dr David Keane, author of *The Art of Deliberate Success***

A remarkable piece of work for Australasian leaders! Many books on leadership set about describing strategies for leaders to implement to achieve extraordinary results. What this book does is it takes things one giant leap forward by embedding those strategies within the unique Australasian leadership context. In doing just this, Jim, Barry and Michael have provided all Australasian leaders with something that has been truly lacking for some time. A must read for all Australasian leaders.

— **Professor Gary Martin, CEO, Australian Institute of Management WA**

This book provides essential cultural intelligence on the distinctive challenges of leadership within Australasia. Drawing on extensive experience working in the region and a wealth of original data, two of the world's leading authorities, Jim Kouzes and Barry Posner along with Michael Bunting, provide fresh insight and compelling conclusions. This is storytelling at its best—direct, honest, unassuming and intensely practical—just the way Australians and New Zealanders like it.

> —**Martyn Newman PhD, author of *Emotional Capitalists* and co-author of *Emotional Capital Report (ECR)***

This book is valuable for leaders at all levels to understand the fundamentals of succeeding in leadership, especially in the context of Australia and New Zealand culture. I also recommend it to successful Australasian leaders making an international move, in order to gain self-awareness of what has made you successful to date, and which aspects you may need to play differently in a new culture.

> —**Charlotte Park, Partner and Managing Director, Mercer Singapore**

This book is both a testament to exemplary leadership in Australia and New Zealand and a practical guide to improving your own leadership. I couldn't help but feel a sense of pride reading all the examples of local leaders embodying The Five Practices of Exemplary Leadership. But we can't rest on the leadership laurels of the few. The authors challenge all of us to step up and become the CEO in our sphere of influence—with practical guidance that has stood the test of time on how to get there. It's a must read.

> —**Dr Michelle Pizer, Executive Coach, Organisational and Counselling Psychologist**

This book is important and reminds us that leaders need to bring out the best of themselves to bring out the best in others. Too often leaders forget the real purpose of leadership and get lost in the details and data. The authors succinctly show the way for leaders to get extraordinary things done in Australasia.

—Luke Sayers, CEO, PwC Australia and Vice Chairman, PwC Asia

This book illustrates why leadership is so critical to the success of our organisations today. It succeeds in illustrating the 'business case' for leadership development and is a must read for anyone serious about improving their leadership culture and their bottom line results.

—Jane Sherlock, Executive General Manager—People, Leighton Contractors

At last! Stories from Aussie and Kiwi leaders for Aussie and Kiwi leaders crafted around an elegantly simple and profound model of leadership. The authors set out to guide us toward 'greater heart, greater wisdom and greater effectiveness'. They have delivered admirably.

—Dr Mark Strom, business philosopher and author of *Lead with Wisdom*

A great read for all leaders operating in the Australasian region. The authors have brought to life The Five Practices of Exemplary Leadership with examples those of us in the region can relate to. They argue persuasively that leadership matters as does the context in which it happens. Read and reflect, and your leadership will be better for it.

—Professor Chris Styles, Dean, UNSW Business School

EXTRAORDINARY LEADERSHIP

in

AUSTRALIA & NEW ZEALAND

JAMES KOUZES | BARRY POSNER

WITH MICHAEL BUNTING

EXTRAORDINARY LEADERSHIP
in
AUSTRALIA & NEW ZEALAND

THE FIVE PRACTICES THAT CREATE GREAT WORKPLACES

THE
LEADERSHIP
CHALLENGE®
A Wiley Brand

First published in 2015 by John Wiley & Sons Australia, Ltd
42 McDougall St, Milton Qld 4064
Office also in Melbourne

Typeset in 11/16 pt Adobe Garamond Pro

© James Kouzes and Barry Posner 2015

The moral rights of the authors have been asserted.

National Library of Australia Cataloguing-in-Publication data:

Author:	Kouzes, James M., 1945– author.
Title:	Extraordinary Leadership in Australia and New Zealand: The Five Practices That Create Great Workplaces / James Kouzes and Barry Posner; with Michael Bunting.
ISBN:	9780730316695 (pbk.)
	9780730316671 (ebook)
Notes:	Includes index.
Subjects:	Leadership.
	Executive ability.
	Management.
	Organizational effectiveness.
Other Authors/Contributors:	Posner, Barry Z., author.
	Bunting, Michael, author.
Dewey Number:	658.4092

Cover design by Wiley

Photo of Michael Bunting: Anthony Burns

Photos of James Kouzes and Barry Posner: John Brennan

Printed in Singapore by C.O.S. Printers Pte Ltd

10 9 8 7 6 5 4 3 2 1

Disclaimer

The material in this publication is of the nature of general comment only, and does not represent professional advice. It is not intended to provide specific guidance for particular circumstances and it should not be relied on as the basis for any decision to take action or not take action on any matter which it covers. Readers should obtain professional advice where appropriate, before making any such decision. To the maximum extent permitted by law, the authors and publisher disclaim all responsibility and liability to any person, arising directly or indirectly from any person taking or not taking action based on the information in this publication.

Contents

Introduction:
The Leadership Challenge in Australasia

Michael Bunting
Founder of WorkSmart Australia

AFTER 21 YEARS OF ADVANCED psychological and mindfulness study and practice, starting and running three successful companies, coaching and training thousands of people, and a lifetime dedicated to learning and teaching leadership, the greatest lesson I've learned about leadership is this: it is profoundly difficult to lead really well. And after more than a decade of coaching and training leaders in Australia and New Zealand, I can tell you this: leadership in our region poses unique cultural challenges.

This is true for many reasons, not the least of which is the 'tall poppy syndrome', which permeates the culture and goes a long way towards explaining why Australians and New Zealanders tend to mark their leaders 13 to 20 percentiles lower on leadership assessments compared to what's reported around the globe.[1] According to *The Australian National Dictionary*, a tall poppy is, 'a person who is conspicuously successful, frequently one whose distinction, rank, or wealth attracts envious notice or hostility'.[2] *The Penguin Book of Australian Slang* describes a tall poppy as a 'very important or influential person, or person with status, often held in contempt by others who try to bring about this person's downfall or ruin'.[3]

Australians are fiercely egalitarian. This is evidenced in many ways, including the informal way of speaking with each other across hierarchies. In a famous example, when cricketer Dennis Lillee met the Queen of England, he greeted her with a handshake and a friendly, 'G'day, how ya goin'?'[4]

New Zealanders also prefer an approach that is less hierarchical. As Rodger Spiller—a colleague and expert in New Zealand leadership—explains, Kiwis often want 'a more collaborative, inclusive, and participatory approach with engagement and real consultation rather than strict autocratic and bureaucratic leadership with dictatorial edicts'.[5]

Consequently, the worst thing Australasian leaders can do is to 'pull rank'—that is, to assert authority based on title or position. It's counter-productive. The managing director of one of my Australian clients, for example, told me a story that illustrates this point well. When his company tried to implement customer-relationship management software for its sales force, it met with a lot of resistance. It required considerable time, effort and a change in management skills to get this done. It was a major project. But when the company went to a country in Asia to do the exact same thing, it was done in an hour. Everyone in that vastly different culture simply accepted the mandate from the top and got on with it.

In many ways, the Australasian attitude is actually a good thing: it means leaders must lead on the basis of authentic values, skills and behaviours, rather than simply depending on their title to get things done. In short, Australasian leaders must actually lead and serve, rather than issue commands and expect that they will be routinely followed. They must *earn* their leadership authority, rather than having it bestowed upon them by virtue of their position.

On the other hand, this way of thinking also means that, simply by virtue of holding a leadership position, you probably have one strike against you. In *every* culture, respect and trust certainly have to be earned. But in few other places in the world will you find such an active distrust towards people in leadership positions. So here, not only are you struggling with the fundamental leadership challenges that every leader in every culture faces, you are also struggling against a deeply ingrained cultural bias.

This cultural bias has its roots in Australia's history as a convict colony. In the founding era, convicts were treated incredibly cruelly and deprived of their basic human rights by authorities. Members of the convict class were prevented from serving in civic positions, which were reserved for the Exclusives (non-convicts). They were also excluded from receiving land grants offered to free immigrants. Australia became an egalitarian society because its second-class citizens refused to accept that they were in any way inferior.[6]

Two more sad chapters in our history are worth mentioning: the Stolen Generations and the Forgotten Australians. Between 1909 and 1969 it was the government's policy to forcibly remove Aboriginal children from their homes and families. It is estimated that 100 000 children were removed in this period. Geoff Aigner and Liz Skelton write in their book, *The Australian Leadership Paradox*:

> [t]he nation which began through a process of 'forced removal' by authority in the United Kingdom in turn forcibly removed Indigenous children from their families and Indigenous people from their own land. The jailed whites became the de facto jailers of black Australia. Abuse of power and authority lingers like a ghost and has repeated over time and culture.[7]

The Forgotten Australians are the 500 000 children who were removed from their families in the UK between 1920 and 1960 and placed in Australian institutions or foster care. Their egregious abuse is well documented. As Geoff and Liz explain:

> This failure of authority to fulfil its core role of providing protection, direction and order has been part of the Australian story for a long time.[8]

This explains why people are so sensitive to abuse by authorities. One client company bussed its entire organisation to an offsite company event. At the end of the day they were all supposed to catch the bus back to the office. But a few members of the executive team had arranged for taxis, paid for by the company, to take only them back to the office. I witnessed the dissonance and strife this caused in their culture because this was viewed as a total abuse of authority. We're not okay with senior leaders acting above others. It compounds the story of 'us versus them'.

In contrast to this experience, one day I walked into Macquarie Bank to meet with Peter Maher, former managing director of the Banking and Finance Services division, and a client of mine. The bank had created a totally open floor plan using active work stations.

In the middle of the division I saw Peter sitting at a desk. Right next to him, working away, was a junior employee. It made Peter accessible, normal, one of the team. If he needed to make or take confidential calls, there were private rooms he could pop into. This is one of the reasons why he was so loved in his organisation. Now, don't take from this that I'm insinuating that having offices is wrong. That's not the point. The point is that, as a leader, connecting as a human being on equal footing with your team members is crucial.

It's because of our history that we both distrust authority and we are leery of taking on authority roles for fear of how we will be perceived by our peers. When I interviewed Geoff Aigner for his insights into the modern-day challenges of applying leadership practices in our region, his immediate response was, 'It's our ambivalence around power. When it comes to taking on roles of authority or leadership here, people want it and don't want it at the same time'.

Rich Hirst, a director at CEO Forum Group — which provides services to CEOs, CFOs and HR directors leading the Australian subsidiary of foreign-owned multinationals — echoes this:

> We don't like to grandstand here and it tends not to be well received by others. This is related to that 'tall poppy' dynamic, an unspoken national ethos whereby those that assume authority risk being cut down to the same size as others. Successful executives in Australia tend to lead more collegially, combining mateship with humility while providing a compelling and clear vision of the future to benefit all.

Obviously, this dynamic creates a dilemma because when people think about providing leadership, and even stepping into official leadership positions and roles, they are hesitant to assert leadership.

They can be reluctant to hold people accountable for fear of disrupting relationships.[9]

It's also interesting to note that Australians on the one hand take great pride in their 'fair dinkum' honesty (we say that we tell it like it is). People are tremendously sensitive to 'bull' or inauthenticity. Yet, paradoxically, there is a subtle cultural norm to avoid confrontation, to circumvent blame and to evade taking personal responsibility, deferring to collective responsibility. Shaun McCarthy, Chairman of Human Synergistics in Australia and New Zealand, provides an example of this phenomenon:

> So, if I'm sitting in a meeting with you and I disagree with something you say, I won't always challenge you openly, but I might sigh and roll my eyes. We behave in a way that is non-supportive and non-constructive in an aggressive manner, but we use passive strategies to do it.

In other words, while honesty and authenticity are valued deeply, people often skirt issues or, when it comes to leadership, display honesty in a passive-aggressive way. As Geoff Aigner puts it, 'I think we are more straight with each other when our power is equal (or we think it is). But we have a hard time speaking upwards in hierarchies'.

Exemplary leaders who are sensitive to these cultural issues in our region facilitate honesty by welcoming and encouraging direct feedback from team members. They walk a fine line between being 'one of the mates' and exhibiting strong leadership. As Nathalie McNeil, HR Director for Novartis Australia, explains:

> Here you've got to be humble. You have to become part of the team. You know you've arrived here when people 'take the piss

out of you'—when they start teasing you. You win people over when you admit mistakes and show your humanity.

Rich Hirst says the key is to never act from ego:

> I think what the successful leaders here tend to do is balance that direct conversation with the skills and ability to articulate it in a fashion that's not coming across as being ego-driven.

New Zealanders tend to value modesty and to distrust those who talk about their own merits, explains Chellie Spiller, a leadership expert based at the University of Auckland Business School and co-editor of the book *Authentic Leadership*.[10] Being humble is a quality also valued in Māori leaders, says Chellie. A popular Māori proverb, 'kāore te kūmara e whaakii ana tana reka', translates as 'the sweet potato does not say how sweet it is'.

Shaun McCarthy concurs that 'New Zealanders really do embrace humility'. For example, he says, 'When Wellington City won the "coolest little capital in the world" award, the headline in the newspaper was "We're not really that cool, are we?"'

Clearly, a directive style does not work very effectively in either culture. But the truth is this: no matter how much people distrust authority and no matter how egalitarian they proclaim to be, everyone craves leadership. People want to feel that others care about them. They want to be engaged in a project, a goal, a vision bigger than themselves. They want to perform at their best. They want to make meaningful contributions to their organisations, their teams and their customers. They want to be appreciated and valued for who they are and what they contribute. And facilitating all of this requires leadership.

That's what this book is about: how to practise leadership in the most effective manner—particularly within the Australasian culture—in a way that engages people and drives performance. Thankfully, my partners and friends Jim Kouzes and Barry Posner, authors of many best-selling books on leadership, including *The Leadership Challenge: How to Make Extraordinary Things Happen in Organizations*, have created a research-based framework for leadership that works in any culture, for any organisation. Their research, methodology and leadership practices provide the basis of both this book and our leadership development work in this region.

Both have strong roots and experiences in the region. Jim has worked with Telstra and Vodafone, and has conducted seminars for the Australian Institute of Management (AIM). Barry has been a visiting professor at the Graduate School of Management, University of Western Australia. Over the years he has worked with Westpac, ANZ, Chevron Australia, the Australian Institute of Company Directors, Bunnings Warehouse, Australia Post, the Public Service Commission and Western Mining Corporation, and has presented seminars in Auckland, Wellington and Christchurch.

This book is a testament to the power and importance of leadership in Australia and New Zealand. In writing it, we have been honoured by the contributions of research firms Towers Watson, Aon Hewitt and Great Place to Work®. They have given us access to expert insights, invaluable research and data specific to this region. We've combined our research and experience with theirs, along with case studies of exemplary Australian and New Zealand leaders, to whom we are grateful both for their examples and for their willingness to share their experiences and insights with us. What's more, we didn't just talk with the leaders themselves; we also interviewed their direct reports, colleagues and managers. In this way, we validated what these exemplary leaders said themselves, and also got the chance to hear and learn how their actions made others feel, fostering engagement and higher levels of productivity.

We wrote this book for two reasons: first, because leadership matters—it is the single greatest determining factor for improving levels of engagement and achieving extraordinary results; and, second, because leading in Australia and New Zealand requires sensitivity to the culture and an awareness of context. Our purpose is to help Australasian leaders learn the mindsets, attitudes, behaviours and skills necessary to make extraordinary things happen.

Leadership is one of the most difficult tasks any human being can undertake. Leadership in Australasia poses unique challenges. But it *can* be done. More directly, *you* can do it. The wish that Jim, Barry and I have is that this book will help you do it with greater heart, greater wisdom and greater effectiveness.

Chapter 1

Exemplary leadership: creating high engagement and extraordinary results

WHETHER YOU ARE WORKING in an 80-year-old corporate icon, a high-tech start-up with the ink still wet on the incorporation papers, a government department, a small business, a family-owned enterprise or a non-profit agency, there is no shortage of leadership challenges. Trust in corporations, the government and institutions in general keeps eroding, and there's no indication that this trend is going to change direction anytime soon. Besides that, employee commitment and engagement have taken a dip, and many of the people who are still employed are indicating that they would jump ship if they got the chance. There's no doubt about it: we live in turbulent and uncertain times.

As surprising as it may sound, in these uncertain and difficult times we're likely to see some of the most extraordinary leadership we've seen in decades. Leaders, it turns out, don't perform at their best when they're maintaining the status quo or when they feel comfortable. They perform best when faced with adversity, crises, setbacks and great difficulty. Challenge is the opportunity for greatness.[1]

Extraordinary results can only come about from doing things that have not been done before. The key is to create a workplace characterised by high levels of employee engagement and commitment. This doesn't happen without leadership. Indeed, as the late management guru Peter Drucker so aptly observed, 'Only three things happen naturally in organisations: friction, confusion and underperformance. Everything else requires leadership'. There is overwhelming evidence that exemplary leadership drives engagement, and in turn, high engagement creates extraordinary organisational results.[2] So if you want better results for your organisation, ensure that you are working on providing and fostering exemplary leadership within it.

Our evidence shows that exemplary leadership makes a significant difference in people's engagement at work and in the performance of their organisations. We'll explore what the difference looks like in terms of The Five Practices of Exemplary Leadership® — the practices that we've found through our research lead to extraordinary results. And within this framework we will provide you with practical ideas and actions you can take to become a better leader and foster a great workplace. And all of this will be explored within the context of Australasian culture, people, places, relationships and organisations.

Leadership makes a difference

Consider what people report when we ask them to think about either the worst or the best leader they have ever worked for and the percentage of their talents that each leader utilised.[3] We've asked this question of a wide variety of people, including senior HR executives, graduate students in higher education administration, marketing executives with a global cosmetics firm, palliative medicine physicians, mining managers and operators, software engineers, financial analysts and community organisers. Their answers have been quite consistent. When we asked people to think about their worst leaders by saying, 'Give us a number from 1 to 100', we got a range of answers between 2 and 40 per cent, with an average of about 31 per cent. In other words, our research shows that people report that, in their experience, their worst leaders tapped less than one-third of their available energy and talents. Many continued to work hard, but few said they put into their work all that they were capable of delivering. Those few who reported a higher percentage voiced resentment about how they had to do so much more than was really necessary because of their boss's ineptitude and lack of leadership.

This percentage is in sharp contrast to what people report when they think about their most admired leader. The best leaders bring out anywhere between 40 per cent of people's talents (this bottom was the top of the range for the worst leaders!) and 100 per cent; and, in fact, many people say that these leaders procure more than 100 per cent of their talents! We know that it's mathematically impossible to deliver more than 100 per cent of one's talents, yet people shake their heads and say, 'No, that leader really did get me to do more than I believed I was capable of doing or thought was possible'.

There's clearly a difference between our best and our worst leaders. As illustrated in figure 1.1, the best leaders get more than three times the amount of talent, energy, commitment and motivation from people than their counterparts at the other end of the spectrum.[4]

Figure 1.1: the best leaders bring out two to three times more talent in others than the worst leaders

Our data on employee engagement reinforces the experience that people have when thinking about their best and worst leaders. In analysing responses from more than two million people around the world, we've found that those leaders who more frequently exhibit The Five Practices of Exemplary Leadership have employees who are significantly more committed, proud, motivated, loyal and productive than those who work with leaders who engage in these practices less frequently. Overall engagement scores are 25 to 50 per cent higher among the groups with leaders who exhibit exemplary leadership.[5]

When people reflect on their own experiences, it becomes crystal clear that leadership makes a difference. The way leaders behave makes a tangible and meaningful difference in people's willingness to put forward more discretionary effort in the work they are doing, and this, in turn, results in higher levels of organisational productivity and profitability.

Are leaders born or made?

If leaders make a difference, is it really possible to develop leaders who can make a difference? Isn't talent fixed, and people either have it or they don't? We hear this all the time. In nearly every class we teach or speech we give, someone invariably asks, 'Are leaders born or made?'

When asked this question, our answer, always offered with a smile, is this: 'We've never met a leader who wasn't born. We've also never met an accountant, artist, athlete, engineer, lawyer, physician, writer, or zoologist who wasn't born. We're all born. That's a given. It's what you do with what you have before you die that makes the difference'.

Let's get something straight. Leadership is not preordained. It is not a gene, and it is not a trait. There is no hard evidence to support the assertion that leadership is imprinted in the DNA of only some individuals and that everyone else has missed out and is doomed to be clueless.

Leadership can be learned. It's an observable pattern of practices and behaviours and a definable set of skills and abilities. And any skill can be learned, strengthened, honed and enhanced. What's required, however, is the willingness to become better. No matter how much skill or talent you have, if you're not willing to improve or you're not interested in being better than you are today, then no amount of coaching and no amount of practice is going to make a difference. We find in our studies that the more people are engaged in learning and the more interested they are in learning, the more successful they are in leading.[6] Great leaders are great learners.[7] They stay open to new information and to the ideas of others, and they're not afraid to experiment and to make mistakes.

If you want to be great at anything—whether it's playing bridge, playing the piano, playing sports or being a leader—sustained effort, practice, a tolerance for discomfort and good coaching are required. The truth of the matter is that if you know that leadership makes a difference and you want to be a better leader, you have to deliberately and consciously practise and practise and practise. So, what do you practise?

The Five Practices of Exemplary Leadership

What is it that people are doing when they're at their personal best as leaders? What are they doing when they're making extraordinary things happen? We've been asking these questions of leaders at all levels for more than three decades, and the responses have been highly consistent and illuminating. As far back as 1984 we began asking people in Australia and New Zealand to tell us about their personal best leadership experiences.[8] Over the years we've analysed, around the globe, more than 5000 interviews and case studies and more than five million survey responses from all kinds of organisations, industries, functions, levels, occupations, ages and ethnicities.

The Five Practices of Exemplary Leadership emerged from this global research. When performing at their best, leaders:

- Model the Way
- Inspire a Shared Vision
- Challenge the Process
- Enable Others to Act
- Encourage the Heart.

In each of the chapters that follow, we'll expand upon each of these practices with in-depth examples and practical applications, but here are a few brief snapshots of what people say when they're at their personal best as leaders.

Model the Way

Tyrone O'Neill, Director of Customer Marketing at Optus (one of Australia's major providers of internet and mobile-phone services), shared with us that the foundation of leadership is trust, which he says 'comes from people knowing who you are and seeing that you are consistent in your behaviour. It's only through action that you prove trustworthiness'. In order to mobilise others to willingly follow, leaders must first be crystal clear about their values and beliefs. Then they hold themselves, as well as those around them, accountable for putting shared values into action.

Inspire a Shared Vision

Derek McCormack, Vice Chancellor of Auckland University of Technology, told us that when he was charged with growing the institution he realised that his job 'wasn't to find a vision myself, but to create a shared vision so that we could all get on the same journey together. It's about helping people see how they can establish their place in the vision'. Leaders have to focus on the future and be contagiously enthusiastic about how things can be better than the status quo, and they do this in a way that incorporates the hopes and dreams of others. Leaders articulate how everyone will be best served by a common purpose.

Challenge the Process

Cindy Dunham, General Manager of Rio Tinto's procurement department, constantly listens for people making claims that something can't be done. 'I see that as a real challenge,' she says, 'and I love breaking down the barriers and coming back and saying, "Hey, see how we were able to innovate and make it happen!"' Leaders look beyond the horizons and confines of their own experiences and organisational boundaries. They create an environment where people get a chance to experiment, stretch themselves and challenge established processes.

Enable Others to Act

Trish Langridge, Chief Services Officer for WaterCare in Auckland, concluded from her best leadership experience that, 'You can move mountains if you're prepared to involve people, and listen, and help them find a way'. Leaders realise that they do not achieve success all by themselves. Building trust and relationships with the people who make the project work is essential. Leaders build both the competence and confidence of the people around them.

Encourage the Heart

When Mushfiq Rahman, Contracts Manager for ALS Industrial, changed from a numbers-driven to a people-driven approach, he noticed an immediate difference in results. He said, 'I spent some time with everyone individually and thanked them personally for their contribution. People felt appreciated that I was spending a lot of time with them, and trying to genuinely understand their concerns'. Leaders are more than willing to share the credit with others and find creative ways to recognise individuals who are making a difference. They demonstrate genuine interest in the success of others and bring people together to celebrate victories connected with key values and accomplishments.

* * *

The Five Practices of Exemplary Leadership framework has been subjected to rigorous testing of its reliability and validity by nearly 700 scholars around the world, who have used this model in their own studies of leadership. You can find abstracts of these studies at www.theleadershipchallenge.com. But before explaining in detail what The Five Practices look like in action and how you can get started using them, let's go back for a moment to the opening premise: exemplary leadership creates high levels of engagement and fosters great personal and organisational performance.

Why does high engagement matter?

In their book *The Great Workplace*, Michael Burchell and Jennifer Robin report that when people describe what it's like to be highly engaged in a great workplace '[t]hey begin to smile and they talk about how they are excited to get to work, and, at the end of the day, are surprised to discover that the day has already disappeared'.[9] Isn't that the kind of day anyone would like to have? Isn't that the kind of day you'd like everybody you work with in your organisation to have? You come to work, and all of a sudden the day's over, and you're delighted by how time has flown while you were doing what you enjoy.

In an in-depth study of this important workplace topic, *The Conference Board* reports that engagement is a heightened emotional connection that you have with your workplace, and this connection drives (even compels) you to work hard.[10] Feeling positive about being part of the workplace strongly influences people's willingness to apply discretionary effort to their work. This is exactly what we saw in the research we conducted on the best and worst leaders. People will put forth great effort for their best leaders and very little for their worst leaders. Leaders who foster engagement stimulate people to go from acceptable to good and even to great.

Research firm Towers Watson adds the element of 'sustainability' to engagement, defining engagement as being 'motivated, enabled and energised to deliver my best performance, and *sustain it over time*'.[11] They have reported that organisations with relatively high rates of engagement consistently outperformed their sector benchmarks for growth across a range of financials. Engaged employees behave in ways that enhance product/service delivery and/or customer focus, which supports greater earnings and net income, and ultimately generates higher profitability. The organisational resources derived from those additional efforts contribute to the organisation's ability to invest more in assets and capital expenditures to further enhance the business. Engagement forms the foundation for a virtuous business cycle that grows income, profitability and investments, which in turn further supports employees' efforts.

Aon Hewitt reports that companies with an engagement score of 76 per cent or higher (what they call *Best Employers*) outperform the average company on revenue growth (six percentage points), operating margin (four percentage points) and total shareholder return (six percentage points). However, according to their research, only one in four organisations across Australia and New Zealand engages more than 66 per cent of its people.[12] Low engagement is certainly not unique to this region. According to the Gallup research organisation, a staggeringly low 13 per cent of employees worldwide are engaged. Worse, Gallup says, 'over the past twelve years, these low numbers have barely budged, meaning that the vast majority of employees worldwide are failing to develop and contribute at work'.[13]

Mirroring the research by Towers Watson and Aon Hewitt, Gallup's research has 'discovered links between employee engagement at the business unit level and vital performance indicators, including customer metrics; higher profitability, productivity and quality (fewer defects); lower turnover; less absenteeism and shrinkage (i.e., theft); and fewer safety incidents. When a company raises employee engagement levels consistently across every business unit, everything gets better'.[14] In addition, Zrinka Lovrencic, Managing Director of Great Place to Work® Australia, shared with us that their research shows that the companies ranked as 'great workplaces' are the best places to invest in. Tracking market changes, their data shows that the value of their 100 best companies grew by 291 per cent between 1998 and 2012. Compare that with the 72 per cent growth of the Russell 3000 Index, which measures the performance of the largest 3000 US companies, representing approximately 98 per cent of the investable US equity market, and the 63 per cent growth of the Standard & Poor's 500 Index. In short, she says, 'it's clear that great workplaces have stronger bottom lines and are superior in performance'.

So how would you measure engagement? Scholars and companies measure it in a variety of ways, but to truly measure a heightened emotional connection with work, you have to tap into people's feelings about their workplace. In our surveys, we measure engagement through a multiple-item scale we call Positive Workplace Attitudes (PWA). We measure it by asking people to respond to the 10 statements in figure 1.2 (overleaf). We ask them to indicate, using a five-point Likert scale, the extent to which they agree or disagree with each of the statements. We then array the responses along a continuum (ranging from 10 to 50) to investigate how positive people feel about their workplace. As you review these statements, ask yourself (and your teammates) how much you agree with each one.

Figure 1.2: the Kouzes-Posner Positive Workplace Attitudes (PWA) scale

1   My work group has a strong sense of team spirit.

2   I am proud to tell others that I work for this organisation.

3   I am committed to this organisation's success.

4   I would work harder and for longer hours if the job demanded it.

5   I am highly productive in my job.

6   I am clear about what is expected of me in my job.

7   I feel that my organisation values my work.

8   I am effective in meeting the demands of my job.

9   Around my workplace, people seem to trust management.

10   I feel like I am making a difference in this organisation.

We can't help but think that as you look at these questions, you would want people to say, 'Yes, definitely, I agree to a great extent. I want people to feel a great sense of team spirit; I want them to be feeling that they're productive, that they're effective, that the organisation values their work and that they're making a difference'. It's easy to see that the more positive the responses, the more engaged people are in their work.

But how do you explain why some people are more positive and more engaged than others? One explanation may be that they have leaders who engage more frequently in The Five Practices of Exemplary Leadership. But could there be other factors that explain their engagement? For example, could it be their age, gender, educational level or functional area? Where they are in their organisation's hierarchy? Could it have to do with their organisation's size (number of employees), how long they've been with the company, their industry or the country that they're from? Instead of just assuming that it is the leader's behaviour, we took a look at each of these variables to determine the impact they had on engagement.

It's easy enough to speculate about how these nine factors[15], or variables, could make a difference. For example, take organisational size. You may say, for instance, that engagement looks different if you're in a company with 10 people compared to a company with 50 people, 100 people, 500 people, 1000 people or 10000 people. You may say that engagement looks different if you're in the public sector or the private sector, or if you're in health care or manufacturing or services. Or it may make a difference if you're in Australia or New Zealand, or you're in Asia, Africa, Europe, the Middle East, South America or the US. Perhaps your functional area (for example, engineering, finance, human resources and operations) may make a difference to your engagement. So we added these nine variables to the equation and examined the impact they have versus the impact that leadership (The Five Practices) has on people's Positive Workplace Attitudes (PWA).

What do you think? What percentage of people's engagement will be explained by who people are, where they work and the roles they play? How much of the variance — that is, how much disparity between high and low performers — is accounted for empirically by these variables, collectively or individually? Are you thinking less than one per cent, perhaps 10 per cent, maybe as much as 20 per cent, or even 30 per cent or more? And what amount of variation will be accounted for by leadership — that is, by how people report that their leaders behave? Will it be less than one per cent, 5 to 10 per cent, about 15 per cent, 20 per cent, 30 per cent or more?

We've asked these questions and collected data from more than two million people across the globe. The responses have been quite consistent. The bottom line is that workplace engagement, what we surveyed as Positive Work Attitudes, is a function of how people see their leaders behaving. Positive Workplace Attitudes and engagement are not a function of who people are and what they do. This pattern of results for Australia and New Zealand, as shown in table 1.1, is consistent with findings from countries around the globe.

Table 1.1: percentage of engagement (Positive Workplace Attitudes) explained by leadership practices and demographics across countries

Country	Leadership %	Demographics %
Australia	26.9	0.3
New Zealand	23.7	1.0
Brazil	32.7	1.2
China	38.8	0.1
France	25.2	1.4
Germany	29.3	0.4
India	30.3	1.8
Ireland	38.8	0.9
Italy	33.6	0.6
Japan	31.1	0.4
South Africa	33.8	0.3
South Korea	47.9	0.7
United Kingdom	25.2	0.3
United States	27.7	0.2

When we consider all of the demographic variables together, they account, among Australasians, for less than four-tenths of one per cent (0.4 per cent) of the variation in how people feel about their workplace; and empirically, the amount of explained variation in PWAs that is accounted for by *any single* demographic variable (for example, gender, age, function or industry) is close to zero (or next to nothing). These findings dramatically illustrate the point that what engages people in their workplaces, and makes them willing to apply discretionary energy and output, doesn't really have that much to do with who they are or what they are doing. What makes the most difference in how people feel about their workplace is how they report that their leaders behave. The data shows that in Australia The Five Practices of Exemplary Leadership account for nearly 27 per cent of the variance in peoples' reports about their levels of engagement in the workplace, and in New Zealand, almost 24 per cent. In table 1.1, you can clearly see that, the higher the extent to which people report their leaders engaging in The Five Practices, the more positive their workplace attitudes are. This conclusion echoes what Zrinka Lovrencic, from Great Place to Work Australia, has found: 'Of all the various factors we measure that influence engagement, leadership is by far the single most important factor'.

Interestingly enough, when we ask people to rate the *effectiveness* of their leaders, their assessments are clearly related to how frequently they are seen as engaging in The Five Practices of Exemplary Leadership. As shown in table 1.2 (overleaf), those seen as least effective as leaders (low) are reported as engaging in The Five Practices significantly less often than those evaluated as moderately effective (average). And those evaluated as moderately effective are, in turn, seen as engaging in The Five Practices as significantly less again than those assessed as most effective (high) by their people as leaders.

Table 1.2: leaders' effectiveness is a function of how frequently they use The Five Practices in Australia and New Zealand*

Leadership practice	Leaders' effectiveness rating		
	Low	Average	High
Model the Way	35.5	45.6	51.9
Inspire a Shared Vision	32.6	42.9	50.2
Challenge the Process	33.9	43.5	49.8
Enable Others to Act	39.0	48.5	54.0
Encourage the Heart	34.6	44.8	51.6

*Note: The statistical differences between the effectiveness rating categories are statistically significant beyond the 0.001 level of probability for all five leadership practices.

The fact is that there's a direct, positive relationship between peoples' evaluation of their leaders' effectiveness and the extent to which they are reported as engaging in The Five Practices. And the fact is that peoples' levels of workplace engagement and productivity are also directly related to how frequently their leaders use The Five Practices of Exemplary Leadership. The bottom line: if you want great performance from your team you must lead them. Doing this well, in turn, results in them assessing you as an effective leader. Call it a win-win scenario all around!

The Five Practices of Exemplary Leadership: making a positive difference

To explain why people are engaged in the workplace we have to go right back to the opening question about people's worst and best leaders. More than any other single variable, it is the quality of leadership you experience that explains how you feel about where you work. And these feelings affect motivation, which, in turn, has a direct impact on performance and the company's bottom line. A host of studies has found that The Five Practices of Exemplary Leadership are directly correlated with employee commitment, retention and performance.[16] Across 94 organisations, researchers found that each company's net income growth and stock price performance over a 10-year period were significantly correlated with the extent to which rank-and-file employees reported that senior leaders were engaging in The Five Practices.[17] Actual bottom-line marketplace results stemmed from how leaders behaved and, in turn, how their people performed.

In the chapters that follow we'll take a look at just how exemplary leaders in Australia and New Zealand produce these extraordinary outcomes. You will learn:

- what The Five Practices of Exemplary Leadership are
- what the leadership behaviours that make a difference look like in action
- what you can do to help others improve their leadership abilities
- what you can do to increase engagement levels and productivity
- what you can do to become an exemplary leader.

You will also see how by adopting The Five Practices you can create workplaces that achieve great results.

Chapter 2

Model the Way

IMAGINE YOU'RE SITTING in a meeting room with your colleagues and in walks someone you've never met before. That person stands in front of the group and says, 'Hello. I'm your new leader'.

What's the first question you immediately want to ask this person? Our guess is that it's very similar to what most people tell us. In our research the most frequently asked question of a new leader is some variation of 'Who are you?'

People want to know what makes you tick, what motivates you, why you want to be their leader, and the values that drive your actions and decisions. The first step on every leader's journey is a step into their inner territory to discover who they are. That's why we begin our conversation about The Five Practices of Exemplary Leadership with Model the Way. It's the practice that most clearly demonstrates your personal commitment to being an authentic leader. And it's something we heard over and over again in the stories leaders told us about their personal-best leadership experiences. Being an exemplary leader means you will have to *clarify values by finding your voice and affirming shared values*, and *set the example by aligning actions with shared values*.

When you work with leaders who Model the Way effectively, you know what they stand for—and against. You know their standards and where they will not compromise. You know what values guide their decisions and actions. You trust that they will keep their promises and commitments. And above all, you see them as setting the example for what is expected of you.

How important is it to Model the Way? When we asked people in Australia and New Zealand how effective they felt their leader was, their assessments were clearly related to how frequently they observed that person Model the Way, as shown in figure 2.1.

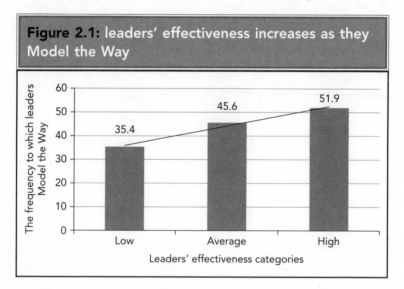

Figure 2.1: leaders' effectiveness increases as they Model the Way

Peoples' effectiveness ratings of leaders were a function of how often the leaders engaged in the behaviours associated with Model the Way. The least effective leaders used this leadership practice, on average, 29 per cent less often than those seen as moderately effective as leaders. The most effective leaders Model the Way almost 47 per cent more often than those counterparts who were reported as least effective. The impact of Model the Way on employee engagement was equally dramatic. The least engaged people reported that their leaders Model the Way nearly 36 per cent less often than leaders of people who were the most engaged.

Clarify your values

You can only Model the Way by knowing who you are and the values, principles, standards and philosophy that guide your decisions and actions. Being clear about your leadership philosophy pays big dividends. Leaders report that the clearer they are about their leadership philosophy, the more committed and engaged they are in what they're doing.

Being clear about your philosophy also has a significant impact on the engagement of your team members. Our research conclusively shows that when people rated their leaders' clarity around values and leadership philosophy more highly, they responded significantly more favourably to questions about their pride in the organisation, team spirit, commitment levels and willingness to work extra hard to meet organisational objectives. Asked about how much they trusted management, the people who rated their leaders as 'almost always' clear about their leadership philosophy indicated trusting them in excess of 66 per cent more often than those who said their leaders are 'almost never' clear. In addition, we asked people to rate the effectiveness of their leader. Those who said their leaders had a clear leadership philosophy evaluated them as 40 per cent more effective than those whose saw their leaders as not very clear about their leadership philosophy.

The evidence documents that, to be most effective, all leaders must find their authentic voice. When you have clarified your values and found your voice, you will have the inner confidence necessary to express ideas, choose a direction, make tough decisions, act with determination and be able to take charge of your life rather than impersonating others.

It's not surprising that work is more fulfilling and rewarding when it's consistent with one's values. This clarity also transforms the workplace — team members report being significantly more engaged as a direct function of their leader's self-awareness about values and standards. Think about what it means to be working for someone who is clear about what they stand for — or not. People are more focused and positive about their workplace when they work with leaders who know what they stand for and what they are willing to do, and who hold themselves and others accountable.

This finding was driven home when we spoke with a colleague of Mike McGrath, Managing Partner of Clients and Markets in Australia for PricewaterhouseCoopers (PwC). His colleague described the impact on her of the way Mike treated the individual who had brought them coffee at her initial job interview: he looked him in the eye, addressed him by his first name and thanked him for his service. It was obvious to her that this behaviour was genuine.

'Mike sincerely saw that person as an equal and demonstrated it by the way he treated him,' she said. 'Observing how Mike treated this person stood out to me far more than any business discussions we had that day.' She also told us that the interview questions Mike asked her demonstrated his own very deep and meaningful value system: 'His insightful questions revealed him to be a very honest and authentic person who genuinely cared about the people he worked with'.

When we interviewed Mike, it was quite noticeable that he spoke in terms of 'we' and 'us' rather than 'me' and 'I'. 'All of us have special talents and abilities, and they're all just different,' he explained. 'I don't think in terms of a hierarchy; we all just have different roles. We're all on a team together.' This sentiment explains why when one of his team members wanted to organise an event promoting equality for gay professionals, the very first person she thought about asking for help was Mike. 'I know how deeply he values equality for all and for honouring who people are,' she said.

Mike's commitment to equality is a genuine expression of his core values. This is the spirit of Model the Way: clarify your values, communicate them to your team and then live in accordance with them. Articulating your values and beliefs clearly gives your team a framework for understanding what's important. It guides them to make the right decisions. Just as the North Star guides sailors, your values keep you on course.

Another of Mike's colleagues told us that he once asked Mike where he found his confidence. Mike told him, 'I very regularly look myself in the mirror and say, "What is it about this guy that is important to others?" I remind myself of my strengths and opportunities. Absolutely, I'm vulnerable like you; this is how I rediscover my confidence'. Mike has a well-defined leadership philosophy, with standards that he communicates and lives by. He demonstrates, as exemplary leaders do, in everything he does that the first step in getting others to engage with and follow you is to know and live your values.

Like Mike, Peter Maher has a strong set of values and convictions. Hired to help Macquarie Bank invest in retail financial services, Peter was faced, at one point, with balancing his core value of genuinely caring for people with the difficult but necessary retrenchment necessitated by global economic circumstances. Ultimately, Peter realised that the retrenchment need not violate his core values — in fact, if done correctly, it could be a *demonstration* of his core values. If the company wasn't profitable, they couldn't take care of their people or their clients. Making those tough decisions would ultimately be in the best interest of everyone. Peter realised that, under the circumstances, the best thing he could do to show he cared was to be completely honest and upfront throughout the process (another core value of his) — to not avoid the truth, but to treat his staff with respect and intelligence (still another core value), acknowledging both the importance of the team and the reality of the situation. Indeed, as Peter and other exemplary leaders have learned, being clear about your values actually helps in making the toughest decisions. Just before Peter was hired, the retail component of Macquarie Bank's business lost $25 million on revenues of $169 million; and a dozen years later they were doing $1.35 billion in revenues, with profits exceeding $335 million.

Affirm shared values

While it's important for leaders to know their personal values and leadership philosophy, they must be careful not to impose these upon others. For leaders to shape and guide the culture within an organisation effectively, values must be co-created and shared.[1] As teams align around shared values, engagement and performance increase.

Every member of a team has their own personal values. Leaders honour those individual values, while building on common values. Those common values give team members a framework—a guide for making decisions. They determine standards of performance and define what constitutes acceptable and unacceptable behaviour.

As Stephen Hickey, Partner and Employee Engagement Leader for Australia and New Zealand at global HR consultancy Aon Hewitt, told us: 'In our work with clients we commonly see three shortcomings on the part of organisations and their leaders. The first is when leaders don't lead by example or walk their own talk. The second is tolerating underperformance and behaviours that are misaligned with the organisation's standards, expectations and values. The third is a failure to connect all leaders and their teams to a small number of high-impact organisational priorities'.

Australasians care deeply about values — even more so, according to research by Towers Watson, than other regions across the globe. 'Company values' rank among the three top drivers of engagement for Australasia, but don't make it even into the top five in their global findings. The research reports that '[l]eaders in high-performing environments with higher sustainable engagement... drive the company from a shared set of guiding principles by clarifying values, operating with integrity in everything they do'.[2]

It was by leveraging shared values that Ed Beattie was able to catalyse a monumental turnaround at Chorus, the largest telecommunications infrastructure company in New Zealand. As the Executive General Manager of Infrastructure, Ed had just been given the responsibility of leading a broadband network project that was in deep crisis. After three years, the project was $300 million over budget, and it still wasn't close to completion. Costs were spiralling out of control. The business wasn't meeting its delivery dates. The team was in a dark place.

Ed knew that he needed to find a way of getting everyone on the same page and operating as a trusting team again. To do that, he realised, the team needed to be led by a core set of shared values. 'The truth is,' he explained, 'that the company already had strong values in place. But on this project, when the wheels had fallen off the trolley, so to speak, people got side-tracked and thought they could do things that weren't aligned with our cultural values. A lot of behavioural issues were arising because of the team straying from our foundational values'.

Rather than doing a witch-hunt to identify and weed out the misaligned employees, Ed led a vigorous campaign, which he called 'Speak Up, Front Up, Step Up', to re-affirm the core values. The campaign's key values are shown in figure 2.2.

Figure 2.2: key values of the 'Speak Up, Front Up, Step Up' campaign

No spin
Constructive criticism builds trust
We share as much as we can, as soon as we can
No politics, no game playing
Calling each other out when need be
We keep it real

We keep our word
We deal with curve balls (and we know we are going to get them)
Ownership: we take responsibility and accountability
Chorus people are present
We do what we say we'll do

We get our hands dirty
We're a company that's got guts
We don't wait for the snow to melt before we fix the cable
We have the courage to lead
Give trust as well as expect to be trusted
People muck in when something needs to be done

'If you see something wrong, you front up and say something about it,' Ed told us in explaining the campaign. 'If someone says something that is not right that you don't believe, you've got to actually call them on it and say something. And you can't just criticise: if you disagree with something, you've got to provide alternatives.'

Once the team was on the same page, Ed was able to implement the changes required to get the project back on track, starting with completely restructuring the team and the way they went about their business. The culture created by 'Speak Up, Front Up, Step Up' ensured that team members did not take feedback personally. 'Everyone had to understand that these adjustments were about doing business and working together to solve problems,' Ed said.

These efforts paid off. The project had been at the top of the 'critical care' list of projects for the whole company. After 11 months under Ed's leadership, the project was removed from the list entirely. When Ed started on the project, Chorus's engagement scores were in the mid 50s (on a scale of 1 to 100). After the turnaround, for three years in a row, their engagement scores were in the mid 80s. And Ed was given another reason to 'Step Up' when he was honoured with the CEO Award for the year. He accepted the award to a standing ovation from 900 employees.

Ed's experience underscores the empirical finding that people's levels of engagement are consistently related to the extent to which they 'build consensus around a common set of values for running the organisation'. Leaders of the least engaged people are reported as doing this 'sometimes', while the most engaged people report their leaders are doing this at least 'very frequently' if not 'always'.

Set the example

Unless you actually *live* your values—that is, set the example and actually practise what you preach—your stated values are nothing but empty words. Living the values in your daily actions—especially when it's difficult to do so—is what makes the values meaningful and what gives you credibility as a leader. Without credibility, you cannot lead effectively and earn high levels of engagement from your team.

Credibility—as earned through example—is how Mai Chen has been able to grow Chen Palmer, the first public law firm in New Zealand, into a highly respected and influential firm. Recently, as an expression of her values, and against the strong advice of many people, Mai waived $1 million in legal fees to publish *Public Law Toolbox*, which compiles her 25-plus years of experience in public law into more than 1000 pages; in essence, Mai open-sourced her knowledge and experience. She was told this was a dumb idea by a lot of prominent people: 'Why would you give away your IP to competitors?' mentors said. Writing the book was excruciating; it forced her to work every night and every weekend while she also continued to lead Chen Palmer. When we asked Mai why she put herself through this ordeal, she said, 'Because it allowed me to contribute my knowledge of inside-the-beltway to those outside of it. And I've always thought that if you can contribute, you should'. The year she published her book, the firm doubled in size! 'We thought we would make a loss, but the opposite happened,' Mai said. 'I learned that when you do what you think is right and give, it comes back to you.' That's what happens when leaders are clear about their values and are willing to live them.

PwC's Mike McGrath also has clearly defined values, so the question we asked his team members was, 'How well does he actually live them?' Their responses were a chorus of 'Mike practises what he preaches'. For example, Mike expects his team members to be authentic—to be true to themselves, with their teammates and with their clients. 'He always encourages and challenges his team members to bring their whole selves to work,' said one of his direct reports. He went on to say, 'At times that can be challenging because you have your work face, as opposed to your private face that you only share with your family and friends. But Mike is very encouraging with people to be their true self at work'.

Of course, Mike can't expect his team members to be authentic if he's not authentic himself. 'I'm not at all frightened to be vulnerable with my team and my clients,' Mike says. 'There are many times when I'm supposed to be the leader who knows what to do; however, I don't really know. I don't hide that from my team; we discuss it openly and come up with solutions together.'

Macquarie Bank's Peter Maher also knows that it is essential for leaders to demonstrate to others the importance of shared values through their own behaviour and actions. When the executive team made the decision to close their mortgage operation in the US, Peter could have delivered the news via email or even through a lower-level manager. But instead, he flew to Florida and sat down with about one hundred employees to deliver the news personally. 'It was how you did it, not what you did,' he says of the experience. 'I wasn't going to back away from the decision. I deliberately sat on a chair in front of the people and just talked about what was going on.' It was 'a really painful conversation,' he said. 'But the best thing I could do was to be real with them. I just told them everything that was going on. It was interesting that a number of them afterwards, while disappointed, told me how they appreciated the honesty in the way the decision was communicated.'

Adam Hall, a director at Towers Watson, confirms that high-performing organisations 'create a principle- and values-based environment, and operate with integrity'. Strong empirical evidence backs up this assertion, indicating that in the most profitable companies employees strongly believe that their managers follow through on promises and demonstrate the values that they preach.[3] Why this is so, was well demonstrated when we talked with Thien Tran's team at Broadcast Australia. They described Thien, an engineering manager, as someone who is 'never asking you to do something that he isn't willing to do himself'. One team member said, 'During the Malaysia project, for example, I learned so much from Thien about commitment and persevering when things are getting out of control. As a team we watched him put in the long, hard hours right alongside us and we all thought, "If he can do it, then we can do it as well"'. Said another, 'I go the extra yard for Thien—more so than anyone else. When Thien says something, I really believe what he says because everything he says is followed by action. We are inspired to follow his example'.

Align actions with shared values

Aligning actions with shared values is essential to modelling the way, yet it's a leadership behaviour that is not very widely practised. Our data shows that leaders in Australia ranked fourteenth and New Zealand ranked twelfth on this behaviour in comparison with leaders from 30 other nations around the globe. These results are backed up at an organisational level by Towers Watson, who report that Australian companies are 16 per cent, and New Zealand companies 13 per cent, *below* the global average on the statement, 'My organisation's management acts in a way that is consistent with the company's values'. Responses, in both countries, have been going steadily down over the years.[4]

Leaders must set the pace for living in accordance with shared values. If they don't live the values themselves, they have no credibility when preaching them. And without credibility, the values become meaningless—no more than mere words on a page. Tyrone O'Neill took this understanding to heart and demonstrated how important it is to not only lead by example, but also how this enables others to live the values themselves.

After years of stellar growth, Optus faced a serious challenge. Although the company had cultivated a strong brand and carved out a healthy market share, the industry was transforming. Rather than focusing as much on acquiring new customers, the company realised it needed to give higher priority to its existing customers. When Tyrone was charged with the job of considerably improving customer retention, he realised that what was needed was a fundamental change in the psyche and operating habits of the organisation.

At the heart of the program designed to accomplish these retention improvements was a clearly articulated and shared value of customer focus. It created context around accountability and helped people understand the 'why' behind directives. But people were already incredibly busy and many weren't paying this new initiative much mind. So Tyrone turned his attention to changing people's behaviours, starting with his own. Everyone on the team who was not in a customer-facing role was assigned a list of customers and expected to call them directly and go through customer-satisfaction surveys with them.

One of his managers told us that everyone absolutely hated the phone calls at first, but Tyrone's actions helped to change their perspective. Tyrone started calling and surveying customers personally — even after work hours. He would visit the call centre and listen in on survey calls. He would discuss survey results with the call agents. He would go 'mystery shopping' on weekends to get a peek into what their front-line staff members were experiencing with customers on the ground. Then he would come back on Monday and share his reports with the team. 'Tyrone led by example,' she explained. 'He showed us how to put our value of customer focus into action. He got into the trenches with us and did everything he could to get as close to as many customers as possible to know what they were thinking and feeling. He took matters into his own hands to solve the problems that he saw. The effect was that everyone wanted to get involved and mimic his behaviour. Initially, we all had excuses for not making the calls or following through on other initiatives of the change program. But his personal crusade changed everything.'

The word *crusade* can be a loaded one in the context of leadership. It conjures up an image of a strong, perhaps overbearing, leader wielding the sword of commands, backed by threats. But in Tyrone's case, nothing could be further from the truth. His crusade was based not on top-down decrees, but on bottom-up buy-in. He led not through fear, but through trust, which he says 'comes from people knowing who you are and seeing that you are consistent in your behaviour'. As he explains, 'It's only through action that you prove trustworthiness'.

Credibility is the foundation of leadership

What the experience of leaders in Australia and New Zealand demonstrates quite clearly is that leadership is built upon the connection between your words and your deeds. Your words express your values, those deeply held beliefs that provide a code of conduct for yourself and a set of standards for others to adopt. We call this 'finding your voice' and realise that doing so involves exploring your inner territory and answering for yourself, 'Who am I?' and 'What do I care about?'

What's equally necessary is translating your values and principles into action by setting an example. What you do, in fact, actually speaks so much louder than anything you say. People will listen to what you say, but they will rarely hear, and pay attention to, it if it is not well connected to your actions and what you hold other people accountable for. When the lyrics and the melody of a song go together, you've got synchrony; for leaders, when the words and the deeds go together, you've got credibility. And credibility is the foundation of leadership. People will only *willingly* follow you when they believe in you. This finding has been so consistent in more than three decades of our research that we call it the Kouzes-Posner First Law of Leadership: *If people don't believe in the messenger, they won't believe the message.*[5]

Credibility takes on special significance in Australia. As Geoff Aigner and Liz Skelton explain in their book, *The Australian Leadership Paradox,* 'Distrust characterises our relationship with authority and it permeates many aspects of our lives. This ranges from suspicion of the boss to the distrust and antipathy we feel for our politicians. It's more than just a power differential; it's hailed as part of our national character'.[6] This distrust of authority, they maintain, is due to Australia's convict history and abuses of power over the years by government and institutions. The paradox, they say, is that, 'We face citizens and employees who are sceptical at best and at worst distrustful and fearful, while expecting to be looked after'.[7]

People expect their leaders to be honest both with themselves and with others. Cynicism is bred when people feel that you are inconsistent—that is, you say one thing but you do another. You ask your team to do one thing, but you pay attention to something else entirely. Some days you focus on one thing and then, for some unknown reason, on other days you focus on something else. If people can't count on you, they are unlikely to willingly follow you. As the old proverb goes, 'Where you stand depends upon where you sit'. So you had better know where you are sitting (what your values are), so that you won't end up standing (your actions) someplace else.

Are you Modelling the Way?

As you've learned from the examples in this chapter, to Model the Way you must:

- get clear about your philosophy of leadership and personal values
- let others know where you stand on the values and principles that guide your actions
- build consensus around organisational values
- clearly communicate the meaning and intent of your organisation's shared values
- set a personal example of what is expected
- follow through on promises and commitments
- allocate your time in a way that demonstrates alignment with the values and priorities that have been established
- make certain that people adhere to agreed-on standards
- hold others accountable when their words and deeds are not consistent
- ask questions that focus people's attention on shared values.

What else can you do as a leader to increase employee engagement and promote positive work attitudes? At the end of each day, ask yourself this question: 'What have I done today that demonstrates the values that I hold near and dear?' This reflection will give you the chance to review what you've done during the day—in your deeds, in your communications, in the people you've talked to, in the stories you've told and in the ways you've spent your time—to be consistent with your core values.

You may also ask yourself, 'What have I done today that might have, even inadvertently, been inconsistent with what I value and believe in?' This reflection will prepare you to ask a final question: 'So tomorrow, what do I need to do differently so that my actions match my words?' Finally, make sure you take any promises you make seriously—doing what you say you will do is the foundation of exemplary leadership.

Chapter 3

Inspire a
Shared Vision

THE TRUTH IS THAT FOCUSING on the future sets leaders apart. The capacity to imagine and articulate exciting future possibilities is the defining competence of leaders. Call it what you will—vision, purpose, mission, legacy, dream, aspiration, calling—people expect you to clearly know where you're going and to have a sense of direction. To be an exemplary leader, you have to be able to Inspire a Shared Vision. Doing this means you will have to *envision the future by imagining exciting and ennobling possibilities*, and *enlist others in a common vision by appealing to shared aspirations*.

When you Inspire a Shared Vision you engage people in a conversation about what you are trying to accomplish together and why this matters. You communicate how everyone's efforts contribute to making the future better than today. The people you are working with get a glimpse of what lies ahead, and even what is likely to be found around some of the corners. It's an aspirational view, and this vision of what could be compels people forward, getting them enthusiastic and motivated about putting in whatever time and energy is required. And the excitement is both positive and contagious. You and others are joined together in making something significant and meaningful happen, and that sense of purpose energises everyone.

How important is it to Inspire a Shared Vision? When we asked people in Australia and New Zealand how effective they felt their leader was, their assessments were clearly related to how frequently they observed them Inspire a Shared Vision, as shown in figure 3.1. That is, people's evaluation of the effectiveness of their leaders was a function of how often they engaged in the leadership behaviours associated with Inspire a Shared Vision.

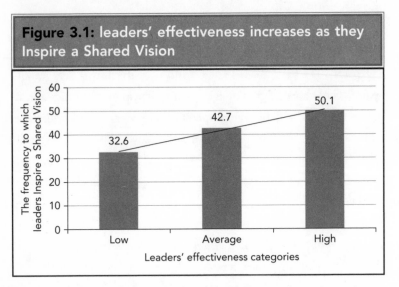

Figure 3.1: leaders' effectiveness increases as they Inspire a Shared Vision

The least effective leaders used this leadership practice, on average, 31 per cent less often than those seen as moderately effective leaders. The most effective leaders Inspire a Shared Vision 17 per cent more often than their moderately effective counterparts and about 54 per cent more often than those evaluated as least effective by their people. The impact of Inspire a Shared Vision on employee engagement was equally dramatic. The least engaged people reported that their leaders Inspire a Shared Vision about 41 per cent less frequently than the leaders of the most engaged people.

Imagine the possibilities

As important as inspiring a shared vision is to effective leadership, it is often the most difficult practice to master. In our studies, for example, Inspire a Shared Vision is the least frequently engaged in of The Five Practices of Exemplary Leadership. And, more specifically to this region, Australia ranked eleventh and New Zealand ranked twenty-fourth out of 30 nations on the extent to which people indicated their leaders 'described a compelling image of what the future could be like'. According to global surveys by Towers Watson to the statement, 'My company has a clear vision for the future', Australian and New Zealand organisations generally score close to the bottom.[1] These findings put into perspective Jan Pacas's reasoning—as Managing Director of Hilti Australia, a premium brand that makes electrical power tools and fastening technology—that when he wanted to take his team to a place they'd never been to before, he knew the starting point was to inspire them with a shared vision about what the future could be.

Jan had worked at Hilti in other locations globally before being transferred to Australia. When he arrived, he found, in his words, a 'very average company', as measured against Hilti International benchmarks and industry peers in Australia. Jan found this unacceptable. 'It was time to create a clear direction,' he told us, '…something that would hold the company together, something our people could believe in and something that gave them the motivation to work together in one direction. We want to be constantly striving for something bigger and better'.

Jan and his team concentrated on two core objectives: first, to double their business within five years and, second, to become a top 10 employer in Australia. Jan knew that simply having strategic objectives wasn't enough. 'I think very often people fail to translate the business rationale into something tangible and easy to understand for the wider work force,' he explained. Jan felt that they needed to translate their comprehensive strategy into something that every person could easily see and describe. 'We're Painting Australia Red' is what they came up with. 'If you walk on any job site,' he said, 'you see an ocean of blue, yellow, green — all representing the colours of our competitors: Bosch, Makita, DeWalt, Hitachi, and so on. We painted the picture that we wanted to see a much bigger share of Hilti's signature red colour on every job site'.

That vision caught on very fast. Travel anywhere in Australia and you will hear Hilti's people talking about 'Painting Australia Red'. When they won a huge contract with the second largest tool hire company in Australia, all employees understood what that meant, in very concrete terms, for their vision: All 140 of their stores would change those yellow, blue and green colours into 200 red tools per rental branch. Every employee could visibly see what 'Painting Australia Red' meant: Hilti's brand in houses and garages, trucks and job sites for all their customers.

Leaders such as Jan realise that for visions to be compelling, people at every level must understand what it means for them. Jan believes that unless everyone in the organisation knows what the vision means in concrete, tangible terms, it's worthless. As he told us:

> You have to express it so that every manager and every employee can break it down into specific things that are relevant to them. The vision has to appeal to people's head, heart and hands. Head, meaning that they understand it logically. Heart, meaning that it's

emotionally compelling to them. And hands, meaning that it's actionable—that they know what to do and they're empowered to do it.

'Painting Australia Red' provided a rallying point, a planted flag that would get everyone excited to be part of the company and to play a role in its success. 'There are lots of people who have no idea where their company is going,' Jan explained. 'They have no exciting future. I've looked at some surveys that show that as many as 60 per cent of employees in corporate Australia have no idea where their company is going, what their future is. How would this make you feel? Would you like to work for such a company?'

By envisioning exciting future possibilities, leaders get people to feel that they're a part of something special. They get energised to know that their organisation is really going places, and not just standing around doing what has always been done. In 2011, Hilti entered the Aon Hewitt *Best Employer* awards and in its first year of entry was not only recognised as a *Best Employer in Australia and New Zealand*, but received the top honour of 'Best of the Best'. Hilti has been awarded *Best Employer* status every year since—an unprecedented honour. In 2012 the company was also recognised for an Australian Service Excellence Award by the Customer Service Institute of Australia. Revenues have grown double digits every year since instituting the 'Paint Australia Red' vision.

Articulate a common purpose

At some point during all the talk over the years about the importance of being future-oriented, leaders got the sense that they were the ones who had to be the visionaries. Often, with the encouragement of leadership authors and developers, including ourselves, leaders came to assume that if others expected them to be forward-looking, then they had to go off into the bush, climb to the top of Uluru or Mount Cook, wait for a revelation, and then return to announce to the world what they foresaw. Leaders have assumed that it's their vision that matters and that they are the ones who have to create it.

That is not what people expect. Yes, leaders are expected to be forward-looking, but they're not expected to be prescient or clairvoyant. Leadership is not about articulating divinely inspired revelations. What people really want to hear is how their hopes, dreams and aspirations of the future will be fulfilled. They want to be elevated by the vision and feel more engaged as team members within their organisations. The vision needs to be tangible and focused on them. This was an essential leadership lesson for Kirsten O'Doherty of AbbVie, a global pharmaceutical company with a large presence in Australia and New Zealand.

AbbVie was created following the division of Abbott Laboratories into two organisations. Kirsten was a director within Abbott when she was appointed to lead what would become AbbVie Australasia. The split created a great deal of uncertainty and worry, requiring significant changes in the company structure. Kirsten had to pull a fractured and anxious team together, calm their worries, provide stability and drive performance—all at the same time. She knew that the only way they would survive in their fiercely competitive industry would be to unite behind a common purpose. A clear and compelling vision was imperative.

Kirsten took the new leadership team on a three-day retreat to co-create a vision specifically for the leadership team. One of her direct reports told us that the spirit of co-creation was something that made the retreat work so well: 'Kirsten didn't just impose her vision onto the rest of us, although we knew she had a very clear personal vision. The vision was built from input from a number of people. We had complete buy-in in the creation'.

After three months of ongoing work, the team finally settled on how to express the leadership team's focus: 'Becoming the new pharma leader, ensuring improved access and standards of care for patients'. They then articulated what this would mean for the entire company: 'We will innovate and collaborate to make a remarkable impact on patients'. *Everything* they did, they decided, would be patient-centric. They sent out frequent communications to all team members about what this vision meant. They created a slide-deck presentation and sent senior leaders out to deliver it personally at town-hall meetings. Kirsten started a monthly newsletter, a first for the company, in which the leadership team expanded on how the future would be one full of meaningful service to patients. In one issue they wrote: 'Our Promise to Patients: "I promise to gain a better understanding of what it feels like to walk in your shoes and use my passion and commitment to ensure we are meeting your needs"'. In another they wrote: 'Our Promise to Patients: "I promise to give 100 per cent in every interaction to impact most on the real customer: the patient"'.

This was not just warm, fuzzy messaging—it was backed by concrete action. Programs were designed so that employees would experience what it was like to have a particular disease for a day. For example, they devised a simulation to help people understand the challenges faced by patients with Crohn's disease. Team members were given instructions via text messages throughout the day to simulate what their life would be like if they had Crohn's. Over a 12-hour period, 80 messages were delivered to each participant to ensure Crohn's was with them as they went about their usual activities such as work, child care or grocery shopping. For instance, if they received a text while they were driving instructing them to go to the bathroom, they had to pull over and find a restroom.

Did the team's efforts at creating a vision and aligning their focus and activities with the vision make a difference to the new organisation? In their 2013 Global Employee Survey, 94 per cent of AbbVie ANZ employees agreed that, 'At AbbVie, we consider what is important to our patients when making decisions'. AbbVie ANZ employee scores are nearly 15 per cent higher than AbbVie International scores on questions such as believing that the company is patient-centric, seeing a clear link between their work and AbbVie's goals and objectives, and the alignment between their work group's activities and AbbVie's goals. AbbVie ANZ won four global president's awards in 2012 and another six in 2013 from AbbVie International. In 2013 they came in at number 12 on *BRW* magazine's list of 50 Most Innovative Companies.

Appeal to common ideals

When Louise Baxter took the helm at the Starlight Foundation, a children's charity founded to 'brighten the lives' and 'lift the spirits' of seriously ill and hospitalised children and their families in Australia, the organisation was in turmoil. Revenues were declining, morale was low and staff turnover was more than 40 per cent. People were uncertain about their roles and their key performance metrics. Clearly, there was a lack of vision and people weren't onboard.

Louise was determined to change this situation. 'We needed a shared vision and the alignment and engagement that come from that in order to deliver the results we wanted to,' she told us. Louise introduced an educational program called 'Get Connected', designed to help each team member personally experience Starlight's impact and see how their aspirations were tied to those of the organisation.

Starlight is the only children's charity with a permanent physical presence in every major pediatric hospital. Their Starlight Express Rooms are spaces in the hospitals where seriously ill children go to be entertained by 'Captain Starlight', Starlight's iconic superhero. Starlight hires professional entertainers—musicians, actors, circus performers, teachers and artists—to be Captain Starlight and then trains them in how to interact with children. They use entertainment centred on positive psychology, wellbeing and resilience as a distractive therapy for the children.

'When a child is seriously ill, it's a very adult world,' Louise says. 'It's completely different from anything a healthy child ever experiences.' Each Starlight Express Room is intended as a 'haven' where doctors and nurses are allowed in only if they're involved in some aspect of the entertainment. It's a place for giving children back their childhood. As Louise explains:

> These children come into a Starlight Express Room in wheelchairs, hospital beds and with IV drips. Their heads are down, their shoulders are drooping; you can see their pain and stress. But 20 minutes later you see those same children roaring with laughter, completely forgetting that they're hooked up to an IV drip or that they have no hair. That's the transformation we effect every day. And that changes their entire experience, the way they handle their treatments … everything.

Parents are constantly telling Louise how important the Starlight Express Room is to their child: 'I just saw my child smile for the first time in 18 months, and I know she's still in there with this illness'; 'The only time my child is not in pain is when he's in this room'. These are the sorts of stories that Louise wanted her team members to hear and experience themselves. 'I want people to get connected and hear the stories themselves,' she says, 'because everybody at Starlight plays an important part in making this program happen. We are all part of the impact and we need to feel that'.

The Get Connected program requires every team member to spend at least half a day each quarter working in a Starlight Express Room. 'By staying connected to our impact, we are inspired by our vision and people don't get so bogged down by their daily tasks,' Louise told us. One of her data managers testified to how Louise has inspired everyone at Starlight, no matter what work they do or how directly connected it is with the Express Rooms. He told us:

> I've never cared more about the outcome than I do in this job. I feel so totally responsible for what I have to actually do for the organisation, and I can totally see the positive impact of my contribution to the overall good. I know that what I do will lead to the outcome and it's an outcome that matters and we can see the effect of what we do.

Another manager further explains how Louise builds a sense of common purpose:

> Louise creates alignment through imparting her vision, through communicating well, through being inclusive, through taking the entire team on a journey, through valuing every single person on that team, and helping them understand why the vision is so important and the impact that that vision can deliver for kids and

families. There is a reason for everything we do. Every meeting, every conversation at Starlight always starts within the back of everyone's minds a conversation about what is the best thing for our Starlight children, and then everything we do stems from that.

Leaders such as Louise get people aligned with the purpose of their organisation — its products, processes and services. They help people see that what they do — whether it's data management, HR, accounting or patient care — matters.

Fundraising is now back on track, delivering double-digit growth, and consequently Starlight's programs supporting Australia's seriously ill children are growing. A recent study showed that for every dollar spent in the hospital system by Starlight, more than $4 of value is returned to the community. Aon Hewitt named Starlight a *Best Employer* and reported that they had received the highest score ever (94 per cent) on the question of how well the whole organisation was aligned with its mission.

Other research in Australasia supports the experience at Starlight. Kenexa's '2012 Best Workplaces' study found that team members' beliefs in what the organisation was trying to accomplish was the most important factor in engagement. Its findings confirm that two of the most important things leaders can do to drive engagement are 'communicate and reinforce with employees the organisation's vision and values (and) ensure that day-to-day managerial behaviours, actions, and decisions are consistent with the core organisational values'.[2]

Our research documents that effective leadership is not simply about the leader *having* a vision — it's about inspiring a *shared* vision, one that all team members clearly understand, buy into and feel a part of. No matter how accurate and compelling a leader's vision is, if there isn't consensus and buy-in by the people doing the work, that vision will not be realised.

When researchers ask, 'What kind of information do people want more of from their management?' the responses are quite consistent. People want, first of all, reliable information on where the company (program, project, product or team) is going. And they want to understand how what they are doing fits into the big picture. It doesn't make any difference where you are in your organisation. It's what receptionists want to know from their supervisors; supervisors from their managers; managers from their regional directors; regional directors from the general managers; and what the general managers want to know from the executives they report to.

If you can't answer these 'Where am I going?' and 'How does my job fit?' questions for yourself, let alone for others, you've just experienced what social psychologists will tell you is 'workplace alienation'. When people are alienated (that is, disengaged) in the workplace, it is because they have no idea where things are going, and they have no sense that what they do matters. If you're dealing with psychologically healthy people who are in a situation in which they feel lost and have no sense that what they're doing makes any difference, they are … well … like rats in a maze. They will just stop moving. They will try to get out of that situation if they can, and if they can't, then they'll just retire on the job. They will do as little as possible in order to protect themselves and stay safe.

In short, the vision must be meaningful and compelling for each team member. Team members must understand their role in translating the vision into reality and have a clear sense that they are contributing to the fulfilment of the vision. As Stephen Hickey, Partner and Employee Engagement Lead at Aon Hewitt, describes it, 'Highly-engaging leaders do a great job of connecting people across the organisation to the purpose, vision and strategy in personal and meaningful ways. They're able to take very big-picture concepts and personalise them to the individual, so that everybody knows how they contribute to the organisational priorities, values and purpose'.

Animate the vision

When Oona Nielssen became general manager of communications for the Commonwealth Scientific and Industrial Research Organisation (CSIRO), Australia's national science agency, she had her work cut out for her. Her job was to communicate the role and value of CSIRO to the public using outbound marketing.

CSIRO has been responsible for discovering ground-breaking innovations and profoundly useful products and inventions including Wi-Fi, Aerogard insect repellent, long-wear contact lenses and plastic money. It developed the most drought-resistant cotton, and seven out of every 10 pairs of jeans worn in the US are made from CSIRO strains of cotton. The CSIRO broadcast the first images of man on the moon across the globe. It is respected as one of the top 10 applied research organisations in the world.

Oona's challenge was that scientists often speak their own language, much of which the general public doesn't understand or relate to. And the agency's marketing communications were often created from the perspectives of scientists, without translating the benefits of the science into themes and concrete imagery that the public could really grasp. In other words, as Oona puts it, 'There was a widening gap in Australia's consciousness about what CSIRO did and how it helped ordinary people'.

Oona's vision was to translate CSIRO's efforts and values in ways that regular citizens could really relate to and appreciate. 'I wanted to let Australia know what a treasure it had,' she said. 'The country didn't know how valuable the agency was. It contributes to industry productivity, sustainability and social outcomes.' Oona translates her vision into 'we'll be successful when…' statements. For example, 'We'll be successful when a kid goes home and tells their parents, "Did you know that CSIRO invented Wi-Fi?"' She says, 'I didn't want us to just be trusted. I wanted us to be trusted because we'd made a difference in someone's life and they could explain what that difference was'.

In short, from a marketing perspective Oona recognised that the agency needed to develop a brand. Unfortunately, 'brand' is not a term that resonates with scientists, and so she was met with internal resistance. She realised that she had to translate her vision into language that scientists could relate to in order to get the internal team onboard with the vision.

Rather than staying inside her 'box' and trying to get scientists and executives into her box, she got into *their* box and sold the vision on their terms. Realising that the language scientists respect is data, she spent time gathering data. Her research showed that people felt positively about the agency, but they weren't sure what it did and what positive effects it had on their lives. The effect, as one of her team members shared with us, was that, 'First, as researchers ourselves, we couldn't argue with the research. Second, we were a bit miffed that the data showed that we weren't as good as we thought we were, and we could see why'. He went on to say, 'Having made us question ourselves and understand that other people didn't share our perspective, Oona got us into a place where we were open to hearing about, "Well, what should we be doing then?"'

Leaders such as Oona realise that in order to get people onboard with the vision, you must learn to speak a common language. You must translate the vision into language that key players understand and relate to. What Oona did, as one researcher told us, 'was give everyone the sense that we were becoming part of a bigger team, and that we had an important place on the team. If she had just said, "Look, this is what I want from you, get on and do it," we wouldn't have been quite as convinced. But she helped us to see our place within the vision'. Another team member added, 'She brought people along on the journey. This wasn't something that was being rolled out from the top down. It was something that everyone had a role in and a say in and she made us feel that we had ownership of the project'.

As Oona demonstrates, in order for you to get others to adopt a shared vision, you must speak to their aspirations. You must first find out what they want and then show them how the vision gives them what they want. It took a long time and a lot of effort, but by speaking people's language and using data, she was able to get enough people onboard with a unified message to begin to make a difference.

Leaders such as Jan, Kirsten, Louise and Oona understand that getting everyone aligned around a shared vision is what stimulates them to contribute as much as they can to the organisation's effectiveness. You have to paint a compelling picture of the future, one that enables constituents to experience viscerally what it would be like to actually live and work in an exciting and uplifting future. That's the only way they can become sufficiently internally motivated to commit their personal energies to the vision's realisation. It has to be real and genuine to them in order for them to enlist.

Are you Inspiring a Shared Vision?

As you've learned from the examples in this chapter, to Inspire a Shared Vision you must:

- understand what is happening in the external environment that will affect you and your organisation in the future
- provide a view of the future that can be imagined by others
- find out about the hopes, dreams and aspirations of others
- enlist others by finding a common language
- make certain that everyone feels they are part of something unique and special
- communicate with enthusiasm about what can be accomplished
- speak positively with people about the meaning and purpose of their work
- let everyone know that they are part of something meaningful.

Think about what it's like to drive in the fog. As you're driving along, you see that there's a fog bank up ahead. Most likely you'll do the following: you'll slow down, take your foot off the accelerator, turn your headlights on, turn your windshield wipers on, turn the radio off, grip the wheel very tightly and focus very narrowly on the few metres in front of you. It's also likely that you're going to experience significant tension. In fact, conditions may get so bad that you will pull over to the side of the road and stop.

Now think about what happens when the fog lifts. You can see ahead once again and you get back on the road. You sit back, put your foot back on the accelerator and start multitasking. You feel less stress. You feel more relaxed and can go much faster when the road is clear and you can see what's up ahead.

The same is true inside organisations. When the road ahead is foggy and people can't see where they're going, they get tense; they can't move quickly and are so focused on the things right in front of them that they can't see the big picture. They need that fog cleared away. The point is that, as a leader, you can either create a foggy environment for people or provide a clear road ahead. The choice is yours, but you know that when you clear away the fog and people can see where they are going, they are able to work more effectively, more quickly and with considerably less stress.

Chapter 4

Challenge
the Process

LEADERS ARE NO STRANGERS to challenges. When we analysed the original set of personal-best leadership cases more than three decades ago, the first thing that struck us was that the situations people chose to discuss were those related to when they were challenged in very significant ways. It's the same story today. The personal-best leadership cases are about triumphs over adversity, about departures from the past, about doing things that have never been done before, about going to places not yet discovered. They are all about challenge and change.

Leadership is never about 'business as usual'. No-one ever made anything extraordinary happen by keeping things the way they've always been. Leaders take people to places they've never been before. They Challenge the Process. They *search for opportunities by seizing the initiative and looking outward for innovative ways to improve*, and *experiment and take risks by constantly generating small wins and learning from experience.*

Leaders who Challenge the Process engage people effectively in the abundant opportunities that exist today to make things better for the future. Turbulence, change and uncertainty are real but not insurmountable. Leaders motivate others to conquer limitations. They inspire people to rise above the norm by constantly asking, 'How can we do this better?' They take initiative and accept the inevitable hiccups that come from taking risks because they view them as prospects for learning and growing.

In our research, we asked people about the extent to which their leaders sought out challenging opportunities that tested their skills and abilities, and we also asked them about the extent to which their leaders in turn challenged others to try out new and innovative ways of getting their work done. The data shows that being challenged resulted in greater levels of engagement. People who felt challenged by their leaders were significantly more likely to feel committed to the success of the organisation, proud to tell others that they worked for the organisation and even expressed greater motivation than those reporting only occasionally feeling challenged by their leaders.

Interestingly enough, these very same results were true for the leaders themselves! Those leaders who indicated that they seldom-to-only-occasionally sought out challenging opportunities that tested their own skills and abilities were, by their own admission, significantly less proud, committed and motivated than those leaders who said they very frequently looked for such opportunities. In addition, as shown in figure 4.1, people evaluated the effectiveness of their leaders in direct relationship to how frequently they were seen as challenging the process.

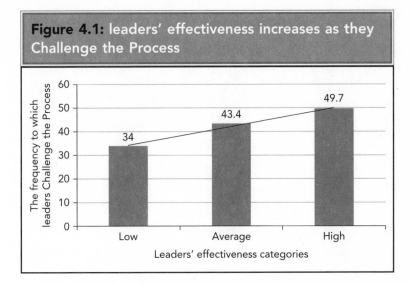

Figure 4.1: leaders' effectiveness increases as they Challenge the Process

The least effective leaders used this leadership practice on average 28 per cent less often than those seen as moderately effective as leaders. The most effective leaders Challenge the Process in excess of 46 per cent more often than those evaluated as least effective by their people. The impact of Challenge the Process on employee engagement was equally dramatic. The least engaged people reported that their leaders Challenge the Process about 36 per cent less often than the leaders of the most engaged people.

Seize the initiative

Leaders are not probability thinkers. They are possibility thinkers. This point was made evident in our research when people responded to this question: 'When you were at your personal best, what was the probability of success?' The majority of leaders told us that the probability was not very high on day one of their personal-best leadership experiences. We were struck by this response. After all, these were stories about times when they were performing at their very best as leaders. However, when we followed up by asking, 'So why did you do it?' they invariably told us something along the lines of, 'because I thought it was possible'. The world has moved forward precisely because some people have ignored both the probabilities of things happening and what others didn't think could reasonably happen. Instead, they believed it was possible to achieve their goals even though the odds were against them. They took the initiative to make something happen. If you ever say, 'Well, it can't be done because it's never been done,' you will never make any progress.

John Studdert is one Australian leader who doesn't say 'never'. He built a successful consulting business, subsequently sold it to the iconic Ogilvy Public Relations organisation, and then served as their CEO and executive chairman in Australia until September 2012. In that role, John saw the need to balance his focus around what he refers to as the Three Horizons for Growth:

> Growth can come from both growing the services that you offer today and from the cultivation of new offerings that clients want or will need in the future. The challenge with cultivating new specialisations is that some of them succeed and some of them fail. You can't always predict the winners. As a leader you have to be comfortable with a degree of failure. It's the price you pay for success. You expect that the contribution of the successes will surpass the cost of the failures.

The path to growth for each new specialisation began in the third horizon as an innovative idea. Then, as it was developed and showed promise, revenue growth became the major focus. As the Horizon Two revenue streams grew in size, it was important to be able to convert them into sustainable profit, and so the cycle was completed. An idea that began in Horizon Three had become a successful, profitable Horizon One area of business. By maintaining a balance between the Three Horizons, John was able to grow the business, with more than 20 per cent of the revenue coming from service offerings that hadn't existed five years earlier.

Leaders focus their attention less on the routine operations and much more on the untested and untried. Leaders are always asking, 'What's new?'; 'What's next?'; 'What's better?' That's where the future is. And that's exactly what John does. In fact, one of his direct reports described him as a restless explorer:

> He is constantly pushing the envelope, constantly thinking, 'Are we doing it right? Could we do it differently? Have we thought hard enough? Let's start a little something and see if we can grow it'. He's always trying to stay ahead of what's going on. So in all our interactions there is always an element of him thinking ahead of where we were last time, and encouraging us to do the same.

This is what Challenge the Process is about: expanding the boundaries; looking beyond current reality to future possibility; always striving for new and improved processes and better results.

Challenge the Process does not require the leader to do all the innovating. In fact, a team that sits around waiting for the leader to generate all the ideas and drive the innovation is a team that will stay mired in the status quo. Challenge the Process is not something that is done *by* leaders *to* their people; it is a culture leaders instil that welcomes and rewards innovation from every team member.

This principle was central to Cindy Dunham's success when she took over as general manager of the procurement department for Western Australia at Rio Tinto, a global mining and exploration firm. In 2013, iron ore—representing 70 per cent of Rio Tinto's 2012 revenues—was experiencing severe market pressure and Cindy's task was to significantly reduce the cost of production in order to maintain profitability.

What Cindy noticed immediately was that although her team had considerable technical expertise, that same technical expertise was dragging the team's focus down into the details. 'The leadership team,' she told us, 'had stopped being leaders and started being technical experts. That left a lot of technical experts, but no-one actually steering the ship'. In order to get them to rely much more on their leadership skills, Cindy moved people from roles where they had in-depth knowledge about how that group functioned into areas where they didn't have any technical skills. The idea was to have them exercise their leadership skills to drive outcomes. 'It put them in an environment where they were a little uncomfortable,' she reflected, 'so they had to count on their teams to actually drive the outcome, and they could spend more time actually leading'.

One of the ways Cindy stimulates her team's thinking is by constantly asking them questions, especially, 'Why?'; 'Why do you do it that way?'; 'Why have you done it that way in the past?'; 'Why did it work or not work?' Or, she'll ask, 'Have you considered any other options?'; 'What would happen if you didn't do it that way?'; 'What if you use someone else rather than that person?' Because her team knows she'll be asking them questions such as these, they start thinking about their answers long before she begins to quiz them. These questions send her team members on their own mental journeys to discover new possibilities. Now Cindy no longer needs to ask those questions. 'When they come to me now,' she says, 'they've already asked themselves those questions, and they've already formulated a plan. Consequently, they feel empowered and next thing I know we've got this process improvement that's already been reviewed or implemented'.

Exercise outsight

Another way to stimulate people's thinking and expand their horizons is to get them to look outside their company and industry for fresh and new ideas. Getting outside the zone of what's comfortable and familiar can spark insights that you wouldn't otherwise receive. Wendy Lenton at George Weston Foods—one of Australia and New Zealand's largest food manufacturers, employing more than 6500 people across 60 sites—takes the outsight approach to heart. When she started, the company had been underperforming for four years. Low engagement levels, weak alignment and minimal accountability mirrored the company's low financial performance.

To reflect her core philosophy that 'my team's purpose is to cause extraordinary performance', one of Wendy's first steps was changing her title from Human Resource Director to Director of People and Performance. Seeking new ideas and methodologies for improving performance, Wendy and her team visited the Australian Institute of Sport to analyse the relationship between coaches and athletes and discover what ignites the passion in high-performing athletes. According to one member of Wendy's team, 'She was able to very quickly take their mental model and think how we would be able to apply that within a business setting, within our own coaching model and framework'.

The sports institute was not the only place Wendy visited to search for new ideas. She told us:

> I'm really motivated to learn more. I read a lot, and I love researching parallel industries to see what they're doing and how that could benefit our business. Sometimes you become the expert in your field and then you stop innovating. I think it's important to put yourself into uncomfortable situations to stretch yourself beyond your boundaries. Making time to develop and stretch yourself while still maintaining the outcomes you need to achieve in the business is a significant commitment, but will pay off in the longer term.

Wendy's innovative approach had a phenomenal impact on the business. The business is now in far better shape, having generated 5 per cent in top-line growth after four years of decline. According to an Aon Hewitt survey, its company-wide engagement score rose by 7 per cent in a single year. But the greatest indicator that it's on the right track is that the engagement score within the leadership team jumped a whopping 48 per cent.

The turnaround journey required a huge amount of effort. One of her direct reports assured us that Wendy never stops trying to improve the business:

> Her very best leadership quality is her drive for continuous improvement. She's always asking, 'How can we do things better? How can this be done differently?' She thinks outside the box, she's quite creative and she's a bit of a risk-taker. These qualities have all meant great things for the business.

Our data shows that the more people view their leaders as exercising outsight (for example, 'He/she searches outside the formal boundaries of our organisation for innovative ways to improve what we do') the more favourable their assessments are around the overall effectiveness of the leader. There's a 42 per cent difference in the effectiveness ratings of those who infrequently versus frequently exercise outsight themselves. There's a similar effectiveness rating payoff given to leaders who are viewed as facilitating outsight in *other people*!

Scholars Geoff Aigner and Liz Skelton suggest that there's a tension between egalitarianism and hierarchy in Australasia:

> On the one hand, we hope for equality and are suspicious of individual progress and achievement, and on the other hand we want to rise above and progress. This paradox can engender 'an inevitable sameness, caution and mediocrity'. Even worse, it can cause leaders to, in their urgency, act like 'one of the ordinary gang' and refuse to fully take up their real leadership responsibilities.[1]

To Challenge the Process leaders must break the mould and go against the grain, which can be uncomfortable in the Australasian culture. Yet the data clearly shows that doing so makes a difference, with higher levels of engagement and increased performance.

Generate small wins

Leaders cannot extend boundaries without taking chances. Innovation is largely a function of repeated mistakes and failure coupled with learning from those experiences. Nothing better can ever emerge unless people are willing to try something new, even if they don't get it right the first time, which is by far the most typical outcome. Leaders experiment with new and different ideas, methods and approaches.

Momentum is always critical to learning, as it is to innovation. 'When you're pushing boundaries you make a bunch of mistakes,' John Studdert (former CEO and executive chairman of Ogilvy Public Relations in Australia) observes, 'but you learn quickly and move on when you can't get an idea to gain traction. Some ideas will work, some of them won't'. To get an idea off the ground, John says, 'What you want to do is to build some momentum around it quickly through profiling success. And you want the first things that get acknowledgement to be the wins. So, going out and finding out what those successes were, and celebrating them, makes a big difference'. This was a lesson that served Richard Hall—Associate Dean, Management Education, at the University of Sydney's Business School—well in developing and launching a new Executive MBA program, an education space the university had never entered.

'The last thing the world needs is another MBA program,' Richard said in initially reacting to this initiative. But, he thought, 'If we have to have one, then why don't we try the radical idea of making it the very best we can? Why not actually design one that meets real market demands, and meets the express needs stipulated by the critiques of existing MBAs?' He explains:

> We realised that our change imperative wasn't, 'We've got to be in the MBA market'—because that market is crowded and poorly differentiated. Let's do something different that the market wants. Let's design and build something that responds to that.

One of the most radical things they did, which had never been done in Australia, was to integrate faculties from a variety of fields seemingly unrelated to an MBA education, such as philosophy, art, music and others. The faculty stumbled a lot at the beginning of the program, as did the students, in sorting out what was happening and how they were being expected to take responsibility themselves for integrating the lessons and learnings across these various disciplines. Richard and his team, however, called every new course a 'trial' and viewed each one as an opportunity to learn. The program's eventual success was due to its ability to build upon these trial experiences as a series of small wins. The methodology, he explains, was 'trialling things wherever possible in bite-size chunks, on a small scale. Failing often and failing fast. Being prepared to be as agile as we could and changing things as needed'.

Richard's experience illustrates that learning doesn't typically happen overnight; rather it's a step-by-step process. Leaders break projects, dreams and aspirations into smaller pieces so that people can experience making progress. An essential building block in creating these small wins is soliciting feedback. When students volunteered to participate in trials, Richard and his team would make sure everyone understood that it was an experiment and that they had to give feedback about their experiences. That information would go back to the various committees, and then they would make any necessary adjustments. As Richard reflects: 'So you do it small scale, you make sure it's a trial, you take the feedback very seriously, and you spend a lot of time deliberating about what worked and what didn't. And then you trial it again and again. With our various modules, we trialled them three or four times before we went live with them'.

Richard pointed out that they were constantly monitoring what they were doing as they were doing it, and after they had done it, deciding whether it was a success or a failure. 'That's the same process we have after every delivery of everything,' he says.

We have an informal debrief, a more formal debrief, a formal debrief that involves the full evaluation, the final evaluation and then the preliminary for the next delivery. We revisit that again, look at the changes that are being made and planned as we go to the next time we deliver it. That is time consuming, but that's part and parcel of a constantly-evolving program.

How do leaders create massive shifts and catalyse enormous change? One step at a time, as Richard's experience demonstrates. Generating small wins gives permission to carry out tests and generates credibility to continue to move beyond the status quo and to learn from experimentation.

As paradoxical as it may sound, leaders make risk safe. They don't define boldness solely in terms of go-for-broke, giant-leap projects. More often than not, they see change as starting small, using pilot projects (model sites, demonstration studies, laboratory tests, field experiments, market trials) and gaining momentum. You try lots of little things in the service of something much bigger. While the vision may be grand and distant, the way to reach it is by putting one foot in front of the other. These small, visible steps are likely to win early victories and gain early supporters.

It's important to note that there's nothing noteworthy about challenge just for challenge's sake. Challenge the Process is not about pointlessly rocking the boat or simply complaining about how things could be better. You have to challenge for meaning's sake. There needs to be a positive purpose behind questioning the status quo because in the end that's what it takes to get through the tough times.

Learn from experience

Jodi Williams, Head of Global Brand Development for Air New Zealand, knew she had to take risks in order to take the company to a new level. When you're a small airline at the bottom of the world, competing with much larger airlines with much larger budgets, it's no easy task to get noticed on an international stage. When the airline rolled out a new aircraft full of patented innovations such as the sky couch, which makes it easier for families to travel, Jodi and her team were given the task of generating buzz around the new plane and demonstrating its benefits. 'A lot of people don't get super excited about a new plane,' she says, 'so we needed to think of a different way to communicate that message outside of traditional advertising'.

After lengthy brainstorming sessions, the team came up with the idea of using a puppet to generate interest in the plane and its new features. In collaboration with the Jim Henson Company a whole persona was created around a puppet named Rico, a loveable, endearing soul with a cheeky and at times naughty sense of humour. The fairly risqué—and phenomenally successful—campaign featured Rico with a variety of celebrities, including Snoop Dogg, David Hasselhoff, and Lindsay Lohan. 'On the Skycouch with Rico' videos earned 91 YouTube honours, including '#1 most popular comedy video' in 2011.

As Jodi and other exemplary leaders understand, Challenge the Process is a way of life within an organisational environment, where it's okay to experiment and they understand that mistakes will be made along the way. Even in less sympathetic environments, the way leaders respond to inevitable mistakes, and even failures, goes a long way towards supporting subsequent efforts to innovate, or not. Jodi describes her approach this way: 'When things go wrong you have to keep calm and not over-react. It's not about laying blame. That doesn't help the situation because your team members are already feeling bad if something's gone quite wrong'. What you want is for people to learn from their mistakes and go on to make improvements—and possibly even new mistakes—as they push themselves into the future.

When you're willing to try to do things that have not been done before, you must also be willing to accept the consequences. Consequences are much easier to deal with when the leader's attitude is one of learning rather than blaming. Learning takes place when leaders and their teams get together and discuss what worked and what didn't. Jodi explains that approach at Air New Zealand:

> When you do a new project, it's really important to go back to that again and reflect on it by asking, 'When we did this last time, this didn't work. Let's make sure we don't do that again'. It's simply creating an open and encouraging environment. Because if we don't try new things, we don't grow, we're not innovating. But it's important to always be learning and always be encouraging your team so people don't get down and become reluctant to try something new next time around.

One of Jodi's direct reports told us about another creative campaign the team undertook. The team fell short on a few areas and exceeded in a couple of areas, so, all in all, she summed it up as 'a good learning opportunity'. This perspective is one she learned from Jodi, as she explains:

> One thing I respect about Jodi is that if something doesn't go right, or we don't achieve or meet our goals and targets, she has the integrity and honesty to say, 'That didn't work, and here's why it didn't, and let's learn from it and move forward,' and apply those learnings to future campaigns and future initiatives.

Richard Hall, from the University of Sydney Business School, is another leader who ensures that his teams learn from their experiences.

He says, 'I tell my team, "You're going to make mistakes. And I've made plenty of mistakes myself. Let's minimise the time we spend looking back on the mistake and maximise the time we're looking forward. Let's think about what we do next time, and how we can do it differently"'. This approach gets people thinking creatively and constructively about how to address issues next time rather than dwelling on who is to blame for dropping this ball, missing this opportunity or making that mistake.

'One of the things I've always really admired about Richard,' one of his direct reports told us, 'is that if something goes bad or there's a mistake, he never places blame. He just says, "Well that didn't work, so what did we learn from that and what do we do next time?" There was always the sense that whatever we're doing now, it's helping us learn how to be better for the future'.

At Rio Tinto they use the phrase, 'If you're going to fail, fail fast'. Cindy Dunham told us her theory behind it: 'If you're going to fail, you may as well do it quickly; then you can kind of recover and get on with it'. And this attitude permeates her team. One member told us, 'We've learned from Cindy that if you make a mistake, you go back and you change it and you go on to the next battle. For me, that's been very inspirational. Having said that, I think she has limited tolerance for repeated errors because she believes we have to be learning from mistakes'.

Another member of Cindy's team added, 'She's never afraid to make a mistake—as long as we don't make the same mistake twice. She's happy for us to take a bit more of a risk. In fact, she encourages it. And if you fail, she never focuses on the failure. She's always looking forward. So, okay, we've got this issue now. How do we solve it? What have you learned from it?' Still another told us, 'Cindy never looks for the 100 per cent solution. There's always going to be mistakes and she is very conscious of that. But her approach is, well, if there are going to be mistakes along the way, let's be sure to learn from them'.

In our data we found that leaders received a very favourable response from their people when things didn't go as expected and they asked them, 'What can we learn?' This behaviour was strongly associated with people's willingness to work hard, their commitment to the organisation's success and how proud they were to tell others they worked for this organisation.

This is a particularly important lesson for Australasian leaders to learn, as data from Towers Watson documents. When they scored companies around the world on the issue of 'People trying new and different ways of doing things', Australian companies scored 10 per cent, and New Zealand companies 7 per cent, below the global average. On the question of having a 'climate where ideas can fail', Australian companies scored 15 per cent, and New Zealand companies 20 per cent, below the global average.[2] In our studies, Australia ranked eleventh and New Zealand ranked eighteenth out of 30 nations in the frequency in which people perceived that their leaders 'searched outside the formal boundaries of their organisation for innovative ways to improve'.

Learning from experiments, mistakes and even failures is critical because it creates a culture that rewards initiative, invention and risk-taking. Of course, failure is never your objective as a leader. Continuous learning is. And to create a climate for innovation and improvement, team members need to feel safe to try, to fail, to learn and to try again.

Are you Challenging the Process?

As you've learned from the examples in this chapter, to Challenge the Process you must:

- take initiative in anticipating and responding to change
- constantly search for new ideas and methods for improving the way things are done
- question why things need to be done the way they've been done in the past
- provide assignments that require people to try new ways of doing things
- be willing to push boundaries and take risks
- look outside the confines of your organisation, industry and discipline
- remain open to feedback about what's working or not working
- ask others (employees, peers, suppliers, customers) for their suggestions on areas for improvement
- focus on learning from mistakes and failures, rather than placing blame
- break projects down into achievable steps.

So what else can you do as a leader to Challenge the Process and have a significant impact on employee engagement? Start by asking those you lead this question: 'What have you done this past week to be more effective than you were last week?' This ought to be your mantra for continuous improvement.

One warning, however: if you ask this of others, you'd better be prepared to answer this question for yourself. Although it may not come back to you the first time you ask this question, by the second or third time, there's going to be somebody in your group who's going to turn it around and ask, 'But what have *you* done to improve?' You'd better have an answer! Be supportive of innovation on the part of others — by doing it yourself — and make available the opportunity to set aside some time on their calendars for creativity and imagination, and ensure that you provide 'air cover' (watch their backs) for them in doing so. Furthermore, make sure you are assigning people tasks that challenge them, giving them an opportunity to learn and grow from taking risks and trying new approaches. Like ripe fruit on the vine, people will rot if left too long in one place.

Chapter 5

Enable Others
to Act

YOU CAN'T DO IT ALONE. This is one of the most important leadership lessons we've learned in our research over the past three decades. As much as we talk about what leaders themselves need to do, exemplary leaders know that they can't make anything extraordinary happen without the engagement, commitment and hard work of others. Leadership is not something that you do all by yourself; you do it in conjunction with other people. Personal-best leadership experiences are, in fact, not all that personal. They are interpersonal. In the words of one leader we studied, 'It's not so much about me as it is about us'. Exemplary leaders Enable Others to Act. They *foster collaboration by building trust and facilitating relationships*, and *strengthen others by increasing self-determination and developing competence.*

The paradox is that exemplary leaders transform their followers into leaders. Indeed, this explains why many people are so loyal to their leaders: because they believe them to have the best interests of others in mind rather than what's in it for them. People won't give their all—won't struggle to get something extraordinary accomplished—without feeling that those in charge care about them and want them to grow and become increasingly capable and confident, taking an ownership perspective on the value they are creating and ultimately exercising leadership themselves.

How important is it to Enable Others to Act? People's evaluations of their leaders' effectiveness were strongly related to how often they observed them Enable Others to Act, as shown in figure 5.1.

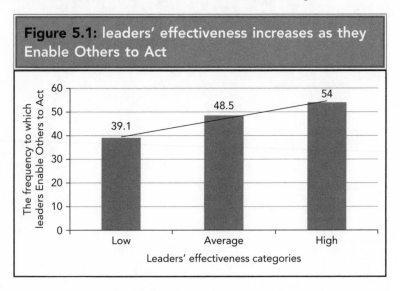

Figure 5.1: leaders' effectiveness increases as they Enable Others to Act

The least effective leaders used this leadership practice nearly 20 per cent less often than those seen as moderately effective leaders. The most effective leaders Enable Others to Act about 11 per cent more often than their counterparts reported as moderately effective and about 38 per cent more often than those evaluated as least effective by their people. The impact of Enable Others to Act on employee engagement was equally dramatic. The least engaged people reported that their leaders Enable Others to Act about 29 per cent less frequently than the leaders of the most engaged people.

Build trust

Collaboration is essential to Enabling Others to Act, and at the core of collaboration is trust. Without trust, relationships don't work, and organisations can't capitalise on teamwork and the synergy that comes from people being interested in helping others rather than just helping themselves. In low-trust environments, people are fearful of taking initiative and innovating. They wait for top-down directives rather than taking action on their own. A low-trust culture is characterised by fear, defensiveness, backbiting, hesitancy and, ultimately, low engagement.

In high-trust environments people feel valued, respected and understood. They feel confident sharing ideas because they know they will be sincerely listened to. They know they can share concerns without fear that others will become defensive. Engagement increases as trust increases. In fact, studies have shown that high-trust organisations outperform low-trust organisations by 286 per cent.[1]

Jonathan Moss—CEO of Frucor Australia, a beverage manufacturer and distributor—cultivated deeper trust in order to pull his leadership team out of a slump. One year when the company was off their numbers, Jonathan realised that the level of trust within his leadership team wasn't very high. The team members were operating in silos and not communicating very freely with one another. Jonathan knew that fundamental changes were necessary. Furthermore, he knew that as their leader he needed to go first. He organised a multi-day retreat with the leadership team to get everyone on the same page. The first thing he told them was, 'For us to change at Frucor, first I'm going to have to change'. He didn't point fingers. He didn't place blame. He took personal responsibility for the team's shortcomings. He detailed where he felt he was failing and made a public commitment to improve in specific areas.

Trust is ultimately about opening yourself up to others, making yourself vulnerable. You can't be sure that your openness and candour will be reciprocated or appreciated, or even held in confidence. You can't be certain that others won't take advantage of your openness. This is precisely why exemplary leaders such as Jonathan appreciate that they have to make themselves vulnerable and demonstrate their trust first. You can't expect others to trust you if you are not willing to trust them.

Jonathan's willingness to go first in creating a climate of trust laid the groundwork for a breakthrough retreat for the team, which cascaded down into the culture of the company. He created trust by breaking down barriers, making it safe for everyone else to share their deep concerns. For example, Jonathan told them:

> I realise my own commitment has been wavering and that this
> must have been having a really negative effect on you guys, and
> so recently I really took a good long look at myself. I asked myself
> if I truly am committed, and I want you to know that I really am.
> I am resetting here and now. I'm 100 per cent committed. This
> is what I want to do and I am determined that we can make this
> a better place and achieve much better business results.

He then gently pushed them, without confronting each person individually, about their own levels of commitment. They all admitted that their commitment had also been somewhat lacking. After hearing about his resolve, however, they were prepared to sign up for a higher level of commitment. 'That one conversation opened the door to a whole new culture of openness, authenticity and accountability,' Jonathan told us. He adds:

> We all realised that we could have tough conversations with each
> other without hurting relationships, and in fact that would

strengthen our relationships. At first we said, 'We need to be less nice'. But then we clarified that it wasn't about being less nice, it was about being more accountable, more open, more authentic and more challenging. Nice is great. Not less of that, just more of some other things, and that was an important change.

By having an open, authentic and honest dialogue about how they were operating, the team members were able to co-create a new strategy, vision and purpose. Ground rules were clarified and new ones were established. One of those was to set a new agenda for their monthly team meetings and another was to create more dialogue to deal with conflict and concerns. 'That's been really valuable,' Jonathan said, 'so things don't fester'.

> We created a new environment where deep inquiry was not only acceptable, it was welcomed. It was about trying to get under issues rather than just flat-lining across the top of them. It was also about eliminating any defensiveness. Our conversations were always about the issue on the table, not about the individual. And there're no 'undiscussables'. If it feels like something that needs to be raised, it's safe to raise it.

A direct report explains how this has affected his relationship with Jonathan:

> He and I really connect and have a great rapport, which makes me feel very open and comfortable. I can talk about how I feel, what's important, what I'm thinking about. And he's very open to listening; it never feels awkward. So that's the foundation where I always feel I can go in and chat about what's on my mind, and be very open and honest.

After a year of the new culture of vulnerability and accountability Jonathan says, 'The quality of our conversations and authenticity has lifted through the roof. The principles and other things we'd signed up for are really working. Trust is emerging much more strongly, and everyone has become much more skilled at both giving and receiving feedback with good heart'.

Jonathan's team pulled out of its slump. Performance accelerated and engagement remains very high. The company has received Aon Hewitt's *Best Employer* award three years in a row, largely the result of Jonathan's effectiveness at fostering collaboration through creating a climate of trust for his team to be at its best.

Facilitate relationships

Strong, healthy relationships are built on trust, good listening and sincere concern for one another. They are the grease that makes the gears of all organisations run smoothly. Such relationships produce an organisational environment where people look forward to coming to work each morning. They drive both engagement and performance. They also help teams weather storms and manage difficult and stressful times.

All of this was precisely what Trish Langridge reflected on when she told us how she navigated her team through a difficult challenge. Trish was the chief services officer for WaterCare, a non-profit, government-run water wholesaler and retailer for the Auckland region that serves 450000 customers. When Auckland Council decided to combine seven customer-service entities into one, Trish was given the enormous responsibility of leading the project and finishing it within 18 months.

The massive change created a highly emotional and fearful environment. Many positions would become redundant. No-one would be unaffected. Trish realised that she could not be heavy handed and directive in her approach; moving the project along smoothly would require relationships of trust and collaboration. 'I put a lot of effort right at the beginning to get to know the managers and team leaders and have them get to know me,' Trish told us, 'and to discuss how we might approach this challenge—because having their trust was the most important thing I could do, and that's where I started'.

More than anything, this required investing a tremendous amount of time and effort into communication. Trish said that she set up lots of meetings, went out to visit people at their workplaces and brought everyone together for workshops. There were 500 staff in total affected, and it took 13 different roadshows to get the messages out. These roadshows were done every few months. She started a newsletter simply to keep everyone informed of the decisions and changes. These conversations and meetings gave everyone an opportunity to share their thoughts and feelings about the new organisation. Trish says:

> We would engage and nut out what the agenda might look like for the next 18 months, and try to gauge how they felt themselves fitting in, and what they wanted to do, and what they felt would be best for them. So I invested a lot of time in that at the beginning, and that paid off hugely. It was one of the most important things I did. We had a hugely successful outcome because pretty much we kept everybody onboard.

Of course, the temptation in situations requiring drastic change is to simply dictate what has to happen and expect everyone to fall into line. But Trish understood the consequences of such an approach. 'If people feel trusted, informed and listened to,' she told us, 'they're going to be far more productive in their jobs because they feel like there's something good happening. If people are disaffected, uninformed, feel trust is lacking and feel mistreated, they're going to be less productive. They're not going to do anything—they're going to spend half their time looking for another job'.

Active listening, as leaders such as Trish know, is a crucial component of facilitating healthy relationships. 'Sometimes people get angry and upset,' she says, 'and you just have to let them talk, and you have to really listen to what they're saying to hear the real messages behind the talk. Sometimes the message behind the anger isn't necessarily about the thing they're talking about; it's the fact that they're feeling out of kilter and they need reassurance'. She explains that she tries to listen to people and read between the lines to understand what they're really saying. Then, she says, 'I repeat it back to them in a way that resonates so they feel heard and understood'.

In addition to really listening to people and attending to their feedback and feelings, Trish remains very honest with people; she doesn't mince words or try to sugarcoat anything. 'You have to be honest about tough situations,' she says. 'Being completely open and honest, and not beating around the bush and sandwiching with compliments and other things that take away from the things you're trying to say, is the only way to maintain trust. Those conversations may be hard, but you damage relationships when you try to soften things for people in a way that's not entirely truthful.'

Under Trish's leadership, the consolidation and integration project was completed smoothly and on time. What this reaffirms, for all leaders, is the value of building trust and strong working relationships. As Trish says, 'You can move mountains if you're prepared to involve people and listen, and help them find a way to make things happen'.

Strong relationships are the underpinning of collaboration and teamwork. Brian Bissaker understood this principle as he led the integration of Virgin Money Australia when they were acquired by the Bank of Queensland. Mergers and acquisitions typically place great strain on all of the people involved, for obvious reasons: roles are made redundant, departments are shifted and general uncertainty is created.

To reduce this stress, Brian saw part of his responsibility as helping people in this new organisation to work together as a team. 'I needed to become a conduit to connect the mother ship, Bank of Queensland, with the new employees in Virgin,' he said.

> So I spent a lot of time taking people up to visit the head office in Brisbane, and also inviting people from the bank to come in to our offices. I fostered a lot of meet-and-greets to create those relationships, and said to both sides, 'If there's any friction in any of this, get on the phone to me straight away because I'll get involved and help to smooth the way'. So I took it as a real challenge to make sure that both parties got the very best. And now we've been able to develop very strong connections through all the teams that interact between both businesses.

Brian was described by one of his direct reports as doing a fantastic job of building relationships with first-, second- and third-level managers across the Bank of Queensland structure: 'Those people are integral in working with us and helping us execute our strategies. We need them. So Brian's not only done a really good job of informing them of the direction we want to take with Virgin Money, but also selling them on their role in helping us achieve that. He's built a coalition of the forces, our side and within the bank side, to do whatever it takes to deliver our strategy'. Good working relationships, leaders such as Brian realise, are central to building high-performing teams.

Increase self-determination

Exemplary leaders provide people with the latitude and flexibility needed to take initiative. Yet doing so is not about abdicating responsibility and authority; it is equally important for leaders to provide structure and clear guidelines as they encourage self-determination in their teams. Before people can feel comfortable and confident stretching themselves, they must feel competent in their abilities and roles. Without that people feel overwhelmed and disabled and they tend to play it safe rather than taking any chances.

This is what Sydney-based Anthony Panuccio came to realise in his role as senior director of support and services Asia-Pacific for McAfee, a global computer and network security company. Too many people in his division were uncertain about how to perform their tasks and fulfil their roles effectively. To overcome this, Anthony undertook a year-long initiative called Back to Basics. As the name implies, his division looked at all of its operational processes and started systematically documenting what needed to be done. The division developed a 'playbook' around four major job roles, which broke down what team members needed to achieve on a daily, weekly, monthly, quarterly and annual basis. 'We wanted to provide a framework around what needed to be delivered, why and how,' Anthony explained.

When asked if the playbook made people feel micromanaged, Anthony explained that the division's intention was to simply cover the basics. 'After that,' he told us, 'comes a great deal of trust and latitude in the way people need to behave and are empowered to drive the right outcomes while managing the account'. This happens with almost every single request that a customer makes. Anthony says that none of the people you deal with are exactly the same:

> So we have to trust our people to interpret what's required and make sensible decisions around which next actions to take—you can't prescribe that at all. They need to be tuned into what's right, and which decisions to make. Otherwise, managers will be micromanaging every single incident we get on a daily basis, which is counterproductive and demoralising for the team.

One of his team members also addressed this issue when he assured us that under Anthony's leadership he didn't feel micromanaged at all. 'But neither do I feel abandoned,' he said. 'Anthony's great at finding that middle ground. I've really thrived under that style because I've been left alone to make improvements, but at the same time he'll still look at my work and ask, "Have you thought about this?" So, we have a continuous conversation about what I'm doing; he'll make tweaks and guide me through in the direction I need to go.' Another told us that Anthony's able to get people to perform at their best because 'he helps them understand what their goal is and provides them with the tools necessary to be successful'. Anthony confesses that he sometimes feels uneasy about letting go. He explains:

> Sometimes as a leader you feel that if you don't have your eyes on it, then the outcomes are not going to be achieved. But I've learned to trust in the capabilities of the people I delegate to. I've learned to relinquish control and allow people to create something that I may not even realise they're capable of creating. And when

I've done that, I've discovered that my team really has the capability of driving some excellent outcomes and developing processes and tools that are now being used worldwide.

Since their experience with the playbook, the team has become quite innovative, with team members stepping up to the leadership plate. For example, one support engineer developed a dashboard that showed how they were performing as a team. Another developed a tool called Lifecycle Account Management, which enables engineers to review how they conduct their day from an account management perspective.

Once leaders such as Anthony appreciate that they can't accomplish anything extraordinary all by themselves, they start to understand the benefit of relinquishing control. They provide people with more opportunities to develop their talents and make decisions that matter. When team members feel they have the competence and confidence to take advantage of their leader's trust and support, they take initiative and responsibility, looking for ways to improve organisational performance without being asked. The people who report to those leaders who are seen as very-frequently-to-almost-always ensuring 'that people grow in their jobs by learning new skills and developing themselves' report being almost 25 per cent more engaged in their work than leaders who are seen as engaging in this behaviour from almost never, through to rarely, seldom, once in a while or only occasionally.

Develop competence to build confidence

Leaders bring out the best in others. When they feel valued, trusted and confident, people perform at a higher level. They discover gifts and strengths they never realised they had. 'The team is all standing two inches taller since you came in.' That's the way Celia Hodson was described to us as we learned about how she helped to turn her organisation around.

Celia had been working as the founding chief executive for a large social enterprise in the UK when she was invited to become CEO for the School for Social Entrepreneurs Australia (SSE), which helps local leaders set up, manage, fund and lead successful social ventures. Shortly after arriving in Sydney, she discovered that the school had just run out of money and there was no new-business pipeline. Most people would have turned tail and gone back to where they came from. Not Celia; she was determined to make it work. She appreciated, however — as exemplary leaders do — that the challenge was far too overwhelming for one person. Empowering her team was the only way they were going to succeed.

She spent the first few months taking full stock of the situation and assessing the talent, ambition, skills and capacity of the team. 'I first needed to know if this tiny little staff team of just seven people was up for it,' she says. 'Thankfully, I could see that their passion was still alive. They were articulate, creative and terrific at what they were doing, but not being very entrepreneurial — simply doing what they were told to do. They had hardly any autonomy in what they were doing.'

She taught the team to 'proceed until apprehended'. This meant, Celia says, 'that you're willing to just have a go. Keep going. Ask yourself, "What's the worst that can happen?" We needed that gutsy mentality of just moving forward until there was nowhere else to go. And the team really bought into that. They found their inner strength'. Once the team felt motivated and empowered, Celia says, her leadership was about encouraging them to be the leaders of these initiatives. They took ownership and responsibility for the organisation's success.

Exemplary leaders believe that their responsibility is to support people becoming excellent, valuing and making the best use of the talent that's in front of them. 'With a little bit of support, a little bit of a push,' says Celia, 'you can move people where they can really lead, really own what they're doing. And then they become incredibly enterprising and proud. It's allowing people to shine'. Celia describes her team as being CEOs of their own work and projects.

One member of Celia's senior management team was quick to point out that autonomy did not come without accountability. She explains, 'You know Celia is there, but she's definitely clear that she can't be involved in all the day-to-day operations. She expects you to use your initiative. So it makes you really step up to your role and be much attuned to your goals and KPIs. She's created a safe place to work in, with some boundaries, but there's a lot of scope within that to be creative and to grow your role'.

Developing people's competence is a necessary step in developing their confidence. And without confidence, people can't or won't do what they are capable of doing. 'Everyone fundamentally wants to be a valuable contributor to the team,' Celia says. 'So if I can get them to see that they can be, and do that authentically, then they develop confidence to be their best selves. So I help them to gain a vision of who they could be.'

An example of what this looks like in practice is how Celia worked with Fiona, who was very shy and had a real fear of speaking in public. Fiona was happy to distribute the name badges at events, but that was it. She even feigned illnesses to get out of speaking engagements. So Celia asked Fiona, 'How can we get you speaking in public?' Then she just edged Fiona towards it very gently. Fiona spoke with a small group, and then a slightly larger group and then a slightly larger group. In less than a year, Celia told us that Fiona was standing on a platform presenting business awards to a large crowd. Afterwards she came up to Celia and said, 'Oh, my gosh, I can't believe I did it!'

Leaders enable people to see that they can improve, develop their skills and do more than they thought possible. They ask questions such as, 'How do I support you to do what you're doing better?'; 'To get you where you want to be, what are the skills you need to develop?'; 'What are the challenges that together we've got to push you through to get you to be incredible in that vision?'; 'What do you need from me so that you can completely rock at what you're doing?'

By empowering her team and strengthening their self-determination Celia is, in the words of one of her team members, 'empowering those around her with a sense of ownership. She gives you that sense that you can take your work or project and shape it into what you think will work. And along the way she's very supportive and encouraging. That sense that you can actually become a leader within your own project—it happens a lot because she has so much confidence in us, and that confidence is transferred to us so we feel it as well'.

Celia and her team were able to turn the SSE Australia around and get the organisation on solid financial ground. With their programs growing, their impact is spreading. And Celia is having the time of her life. She told us, 'When you've heard incredible stories that have made profound change in communities, and you've worked with individuals who are enabling that change, that's so enlivening—that's what gets you out of bed. It's just incredible. Our students and fellows are getting out there and doing it, with the team supporting them. There's nothing more fulfilling to me than investing in your team'. Celia echoes what exemplary leaders expound over and over again: 'If you support them and give them opportunities, they just soar; they absolutely grow and continually astound you'.

Are you Enabling Others to Act?

As you've learned from the examples in this chapter, to Enable Others to Act you must:

- develop strong, healthy and trusting relationships through honesty, openness and mutual accountability
- stimulate an open exchange of ideas
- promote cooperation rather than competition among people
- involve people in the decisions that directly impact their job performance
- find the right balance between clear instructions and giving people freedom to develop and find their own way
- listen to what people have to say and be responsive to their input
- provide the resources necessary for people to do their jobs effectively
- offer training and developmental opportunities so that people can improve their skills and abilities
- let others know how confident you are that they can learn and develop themselves
- develop your coaching and mentoring skills.

What you can do as a leader to Enable Others to Act is to support developmental opportunities and experiences that build the competence and confidence of people in your work group, especially in relation to their next role or assignment. Let them know that you are developing their talents not just for today but also for tomorrow. People want to be able to answer the question, 'Where's this all taking me?' They don't just want to know that developmental opportunities will help them today; they also want to know that these will help them grow and develop over the long term.

It's also imperative to listen carefully to what others have to say and to demonstrate visibly by your actions that their inputs and opinions are valued. Give people tangible opportunities to use their judgement and discretion; make sure they get to exercise some choice in how they do their work. Take some of your team members along with you to upper-level meetings so they begin to get some insights into strategic decision-making and broaden their perspective on what's going on outside of their own areas of responsibility. Answer any of their questions about what happened and why, including what is behind your own thinking. Call these 'leader-in-training' moments.

Chapter 6

Encourage the Heart

OVER THE YEARS, we've asked thousands of people, 'Do you need encouragement to perform at your best?' When we started asking the question, we didn't know what the answer would be. What we found was that only about 50 per cent answered affirmatively. The rest explained, 'Well, the reason I didn't say yes was because I don't *need* encouragement. After all, I am an adult'. Or 'I don't *need* encouragement. I'm a professional. I do my job well regardless of what others say'.

We realised that perhaps we weren't asking the question in the right way. So we changed the question and asked, 'When you get encouragement, does it help stimulate and sustain your performance?' Would you be surprised to learn that nearly 100 per cent of the respondents said, 'Yes. When I get encouragement, it does help me to perform at a higher level'? If this is true, then it must also be true that everyone does *need* encouragement! Sure, not everyone needs or wants the same level, type or frequency of encouragement, but no-one wants to feel that their efforts are inconsequential, invisible and make little-to-no difference. Exemplary leaders provide encouragement.

Knowing this, exemplary leaders are constantly on the lookout for ways to Encourage the Heart of individuals who are living the values that have been agreed to and achieving the goals that have been identified. When at their personal best, leaders find ways of building the inner strength necessary for people to struggle to achieve shared aspirations. After all, if you're asking people to do things that they've never done before, there's a reason why they haven't already done them—most are probably afraid in some way. You need to make sure that you give them the courage to move forward. You do that when you *recognise contributions by showing appreciation for individual excellence,* and *celebrate the values and victories by creating a spirit of community.*

How important is it to Encourage the Heart? People's ratings of the effectiveness of their leaders were clearly related to how often they observed them Encourage the Heart, as shown in figure 6.1. People rated their leaders' effectiveness according to how often the leaders were seen as engaging in the leadership behaviours associated with Encourage the Heart. The least effective leaders used this leadership practice, on average, 23 per cent less often than those seen as moderately effective as leaders. The most effective leaders Encourage the Heart in excess of 15 per cent more often than their counterparts reported as moderately effective and about fifty per cent more often than those evaluated as least effective by their people. The impact of Encourage the Heart on employee engagement was equally dramatic. The most engaged people reported that their leaders Encourage the Heart in excess of 30 per cent more frequently than the leaders of the least engaged people.

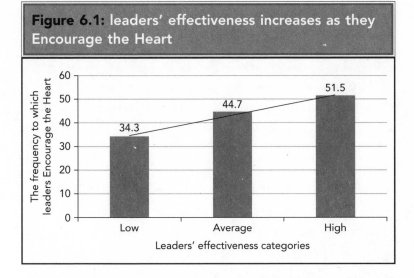

Figure 6.1: leaders' effectiveness increases as they Encourage the Heart

This leadership practice may be seen as problematic for some, given that the Australasian culture is very sensitive to the tall poppy syndrome and the general norm of egalitarianism that often results in people not wanting to be perceived as rising above their peers. As a consequence, compared to Towers Watson's global data, Australians rank 17 per cent, and New Zealanders 13 per cent, lower on the issue of 'management style encourages people to give their best'.[1] Our own data shows that leaders in Australia ranked fourteenth and in New Zealand twenty-fifth among leaders from 30 other nations around the globe on the question of 'giving members of the team lots of appreciation and support for their contributions'.

However, the truth is that tall poppy syndrome or not, no-one wants to be taken for granted and every human being has a deep and inherent desire to be recognised and appreciated.[2] As Rachel Argaman, CEO of Australian-based Toga Far East Hotels, told us:

> No matter who you are, where you're from, your colour, your race, your creed, your religion, your language—we are all seeking

happiness. The thing that impacts happiness the most, no matter which philosophy you read, no matter which research you look at, would be loving relationships. To love and be loved. That's why praise and encouragement are the best gifts you can give anyone. That's part of the connectedness of us as human beings, and any good leader understands that that is an essential need. People need to have their contribution acknowledged, to know that they are making a difference.

Nathalie McNeil, HR Director for Novartis Australia, a large pharmaceutical company, identifies *genuineness* as fundamental to Encouraging the Heart in Australasian culture. 'We have this egalitarian, "everyone's equal, give it a fair go" kind of culture,' she explains. 'In fact, if somebody stands out, we tend to chop his or her head off to say "We're all the same here, mate". So it can really hold us back from wanting to go too "bells and whistles" on great achievements. That's why, here, you're better off not to do recognition at all than to do it with any lack of genuineness. If you don't do it with good intention, with the genuine appreciation for them and for what they've done, then it actually hurts your credibility and hinders your ability to lead.'

Expect the best

You've heard the saying, 'If you don't know where you're going, any road will get you there'. Likewise, if you don't know an organisation's or team's standards and expectations, how can you possibly know what to recognise people for? In short, people can't strive for excellence—and be recognised accordingly—when they don't know what excellence looks like in their particular context.

Leaders who Encourage the Heart know well that it's not just about thoughtful praise; it's also about providing clear standards, expectations, goals and rules. When there's a lack of clarity on goals, rules and desired outcomes, people don't know how to behave and which behaviours will be rewarded. You can have the most talented and motivated people on a team, but if they don't know the rules of the game, they won't engage.

Exemplary leaders appreciate the practical foundation that underlies Encourage the Heart. Sallie Purser, a long-time managerial leader with IBM in New Zealand, is a good example. She explains:

> When we're talking about encouragement, I think there's a tendency for people to think of it as only soft, frilly stuff about being nice, and you care, and you smile, and that type of thing. And that aspect of encouragement is really important because the people you manage do need to know that you care about them as individuals. But I think there is another really important aspect of encouragement and that is to ensure that people have the level of information that they need to understand what is expected of them. It's about providing clarity on what we're trying to accomplish.

Sallie points out that 'there's a basic human need to make sure that you are providing value in what you do. People want to know that they are really contributing to our goals'. How can they do that, she asks, if they don't know what the goals are? 'Encouragement,' she says, 'is about first and foremost making sure people understand what we're trying to accomplish as a team and how they personally contribute to that goal. Then they can really see their contribution in context'.

Because of this, Sallie says it is very important to carefully manage team members who are not performing. Leaders can't simultaneously encourage high performance while letting poor performance slide; it sends mixed messages to team members. If this poor performance is tolerated, what good does it do to reward high performance? As Sallie says:

> If you've got a team member who isn't pulling their weight, you're not the only person who knows that. Everybody around you knows that, too. And if you don't do something about it, then people start to resent not only that person, but also you as the leader. They think, 'Why do I have to work so hard to cover what Joe hasn't done?' So you have to coach under-performers to lift their game or, if they can't, then you have to take the next step and help them consider a move into a role that better suits their strengths. This shows your strong performers that you value their contribution and you care enough about their motivation and engagement to ensure the whole team is making their strongest possible contribution.

Sallie is described as 'a leader with very high standards'. But she 'also gives a lot of encouragement and recognition. So her team knows that if they work hard and perform well, then they'll be recognised, and therefore they push a little bit harder to give their absolute best'. This observation by one team member is validated by others. For example, another told us:

> Her praise and feedback are quite consistent. You know how to gain and keep her respect. You never have to wonder if you're meeting her standards because she is so clear on what she expects. So there are no surprises with rewards, it's just consistent. And if she thinks you could do an even better job, she'll tell you that. With Sallie, you completely understand where you stand. If you've done a good job she'll let you know. If you've got a leader who's displaying those sorts of behaviours, you want to follow them.

Exemplary leaders have clear standards and expect, enable and encourage people to do their best. They let people know how they are doing so that they can keep themselves focused on doing the things that matter and being recognised for doing so.

Personalise recognition

It's clear that people need encouragement to perform at their best, yet leaders understand that one person may not be encouraged by the same thing as another. In fact, personalised appreciation is the most powerful form of recognition. Nathalie McNeil at Novartis says that personalising recognition is what makes it genuine, which she maintains is what makes it effective in Australasian culture. That genuineness comes from really knowing people on a personal level, and sincerely caring about them. 'If you can't recognise something specific,' she says, 'you're not paying attention. And good leaders pay attention. They know their people. When you truly know someone, not only do you recognise them for things they've done, but you also do it in a way that they personally value because it's relevant to what *they* care about'. Exemplary leaders make it a point to find ways of creatively recognising the contributions that people make. In doing so, they demonstrate the confidence they have in the ability of those they work with, which, through a virtuous cycle, results in raising people's own levels of self-confidence and willingness to put in their best efforts.

Levels of engagement in Australasia are directly correlated with the extent to which people report their leaders take the time and effort to make sure they not only 'give the members of the team lots of appreciation and support for their contributions' but do so in ways that are best suited to their teams, both individually and collectively. For example, Nathalie is described by one of her direct reports as having 'a lovely way of knowing when something should be visible or when the praise should be given in a broader group'. Another team member added that Nathalie simply 'rewards people in a way that suits them'. For example, at a quarterly meeting with her core team, she gave out books as gifts for each person. She went so far as to give each person a different book, one that she thought they would have a personal interest in. Inside each book was a letter praising that person for their unique strengths and their contributions to the team. A few months later, when Nathalie asked them, 'Did you ever read those books I gave you?' she learned that only a few of them had. Nathalie says they told her they had done something much more important: 'They had all kept the letters I had written to each of them. It was a very specific recognition of what they'd done, where we're going and why they're so important. All of them remember what I wrote, and they continue to refer to those letters'. From Nathalie's perspective, if you really want to make people feel valued and significant, you have to 'make it relevant, make it in the moment and make it specific to what you're recognising or rewarding'.

Toga Far East Hotels' Rachel Argaman takes a similar approach. When the Australian-based builder and manager of apartments and hotels hit a rough patch, two people within a key department had to pick up the workload of three others over a four-month period. One of these team members described this as the hardest experience she had ever been through. Her answer to the question of what kept her going through that time underscores just how important it is to personalise recognition. She said 'the little hand-written personal notes' she received from the CEO helped her carry on. 'Those hand-written notes are what kept me here.'

It can't be stated strongly enough how much people appreciate knowing that their leader is taking time out of their busy schedule to pay attention to them. While Rachel explained to us at great length why she feels personal, small gestures are so important, the real proof was in how many of her direct reports spontaneously commented about the power of her actions. Said one: 'A personal email from Rachel, or a comment on a Christmas card or on a bonus letter means just as much to me as a public acknowledgement'. Said another: 'It's powerful coming from her because she makes it personal, rather than generic. Just recently, after I'd finished attending a two-day conference, I got a text message from her saying, "You showed over the last two days that you're an incredible leader. Thanks for being you". It was just a simple, personal text message, but those are the things you remember'.

Another benefit leaders derive from being able to personalise recognition is that it eliminates the issue of perceived favouritism. 'Favouritism is caused,' Novartis HR Director Nathalie McNeil asserts, 'by praising specific people for no real reason, no identifiable criteria other than that the leader likes that particular person. But when you reward well, for the right reasons and in the right ways, it's not an issue. When you can clearly explain to people why they're being recognised, and other people understand how their contribution really did add to the team, that risk of favouritism is eliminated'. Indeed, when we interviewed Nathalie's team members, we got the distinct sense that each of them felt like her favourite, and for their own unique reasons. As Nathalie further observes, 'The impact is heightened when you are able to give honest, direct (not easy) feedback in a way that is empowering for people to hear'. In fact, Nathalie's directness adds to her genuineness. If a leader is full of nothing but praise for an individual, it's easy for that individual to begin suspecting and/or devaluing the praise. But when a leader also has direct, honest and tough conversations combined with praise, the praise becomes much more believable.

Create a spirit of community

At its root, the word *encourage* means *to put courage into*. In other words, it means to infuse people with the drive to do something they would otherwise fear doing. Few things give people greater courage and confidence than feeling they're part of a team that shares their values and watches out for their best interests.

Deven Billimoria is CEO of Sydney-based Smartgroup Corporation, a medium-sized holding company that presides over a group of companies, including Smartsalary, which works with HR and finance departments to save employees money on taxes by helping them structure their salaries and benefits. Honoured as CEO of the Year by the Australian Human Resources Institute in 2013, Deven is described by a member of the executive team as 'exceptionally collaborative. He has this real loyalty and commitment to people around him. Once he's made an emotional connection with you, you've got his support for life'.

When it looked like the federal government might eliminate the principal fringe-benefits tax concession upon which Smartsalary's business model was based, there was great internal concern that a considerable number of people might need to be made redundant. While some of their competitors reacted by drastically reducing staff, Deven and his team made the bold decision to neither retrench anyone immediately nor manage leave liabilities.

The decision was not naïve. They were not refusing to face reality. They were taking a bold stance and sending a strong signal that they were a team—that they were in this together and would either find a way out together or fail together. While the decision was seen by some as financially risky, Smartgroup used this opportunity to strengthen its collaborative culture. In order to create some stability during this period of uncertainty, Deven told staff what some thought unimaginable:

> Everyone's keeping their jobs. We don't know what the future holds, but we can tell you that you're going to keep your jobs for the next four weeks as a minimum. What happens in four weeks and one day, I don't know. But we're not going to come in tomorrow and say, 'You know what we said yesterday about losing your job? Well, today you're gone'. It's not a day-by-day thing. And we'll let you know next week where we sit looking four weeks forward.

Each week leading up to the election, Deven would tell the team, 'I know we said last week it's four weeks. Guess what? This week, we're still at four weeks'. And week after week after week, the staff got the same message: four weeks, four weeks, four weeks, four weeks. Eventually Deven didn't have to say it anymore.

To further support the notion that they were a team, everyone was encouraged and motivated to work together to find solutions. Demonstrating their belief and trust in their team, the executive group didn't dictate top-down solutions. Rather, as Deven explains:

> We came together as an entire organisation and said, 'This is a problem for us. Let's figure it out'. There was a feeling that those who are closest to the action will have the best solutions. They're talking to customers every single day. They'll understand how we're going to be able to come out of this.

The invigorated, tight-knit teams across the company put their heads together and came up with an entirely new product, one suitable for their market regardless of the passage or failure of the pending legislation. With the new product created, the teams got busy. They changed all the calculators around. The presentations and websites were all revised by the sales and marketing teams, and the IT team changed its systems to handle the new way of processing. The phenomenal thing, Deven told us, was that it all happened 'with little to no senior management involvement—at least none from me!' Because of its quick, teamwork-enabled adjustments, Smartsalary was significantly less affected than its competitors and still maintained profitability—without firing a single person or asking anyone to leave. After going through the biggest crisis the industry had ever seen, the company, already an Aon Hewitt *Best Employer*, actually lifted its annual engagement levels and was reaccredited a *Best Employer*.

When we're asked about traditional 'spans of control' or how many people one person can supervise these days in flatter and more geographically dispersed organisations, we turn this around to ask, 'What's your span of appreciation?' Since leadership is a personal relationship, how many people's names can you remember? Indeed, how can you claim to be in a relationship with someone if you don't even know their name? Deven has an obsessive determination to know every one of his 340-plus team members by first name. It's not just putting a name to a face; he knows something about each person—about their family or their background or where they came from or what they're doing. Everyone feels they know Deven, and that he knows them. What we learned from the Smartsalary staff was:

> This provides such an element of personalisation and value when Deven's talking to people. For instance, when we had the Christmas party he was the one that handed out the yearly awards to the staff. It's not like he's just reading off something that someone else has written—it comes from the heart, he knows the people and it just makes everyone feel a lot more valued.

Indeed, Deven wants each individual team member to feel valued—because he truly does value each and every one of them. As he puts it, 'Knowing people's names is the gateway to having genuine conversations with them and provides the ability to show care and concern—to really let people know they matter. That's why it's so important to me. It's about sincerely caring about them'.

Celebrations are another way leaders bring people together and create community. Rachel Argaman of Toga Far East Hotels created an annual awards night called Night to Shine to showcase the great achievements of the past year. TFE Hotels' staff come together to celebrate the victories of the hotels and individual team members and share in the inspiration of their success stories. They rent a great venue and everyone gets dressed up. It's an unforgettable celebration that brings everyone together. Mushfiq Rahman—Contracts Manager for ALS Industrial, which provides asset reliability and integrity services—also knows about the importance of creating community spirit. When he observed that the backlog was building and the staff was becoming overworked, he requested a day off from the client. On the day off, he organised a barbecue to recognise the team for its hard work. 'I didn't give a big, formal speech that day,' he said. 'I just walked around and spent some time with everyone individually and thanked them personally for their contribution and the ways they embodied our values.'

Even while Smartsalary was struggling with the challenge to its business model, the whole team got together weekly for public recognition celebrations. The team members would report their relevant numbers showing improvement, highlight individual team members for contributing to the goals and applaud each other's progress. This was important, according to Deven, so that everyone could draw strength and confidence from one another as a team. 'Bringing everyone together has that effect,' he says. Exemplary leaders understand that great accomplishments are the result of team efforts, and that individuals are more engaged when they feel they are part of a team than when they feel they are all alone and no-one has their back.

Get personally involved

When Mushfiq Rahman was put in charge of a liquefied natural gas project, it was going badly. It wasn't delivering on its technical capability. There was no quality control. Teams were not coordinating with each other. It was in the red financially. The client was unhappy, as were all the ALS employees involved.

While Mushfiq had considerable experience with project management, he'd always focused primarily on the numbers to tell him how a project was going. After studying the problems with the natural gas project, he decided to not even look at the numbers for three months. Instead, he would focus his attention and energy on supporting and leading his people. 'It's the first time I'd actually done that,' he said. 'It felt scary initially, but it turned out to be one of those *light-bulb* moments'.

Mushfiq determined that the most important thing he could do was to make his team members feel appreciated and supported. So rather than spend time crunching numbers in his office, he spent most of his time on the job site, which required him to regularly fly from Brisbane to Curtis Island. The first month on the project, he simply visited with team members one-on-one. He would ask them what was wrong with the project and what ideas they had for improving the situation. He would sit and listen to their feedback, and not try to make any big speeches. People felt supported and valued because he was spending a lot of time with them and trying to genuinely understand their concerns, rather than sending an email or stopping into the site for five minutes here or there. 'A lot of them,' he said, 'already had the answers but they just wanted someone else to tell them; "That's a good idea"'.

Although he wasn't monitoring the numbers, he was confident that his approach of focusing on and appreciating people would pay off. He explains:

> My light-bulb moment was that while financial metrics are important, if you get the people right, you'll deliver a successful business and you'll be stronger later for it. And I saw immediate benefits of living and breathing leadership skills over focusing on the finances. I knew that we were heading in the right direction, and that it would eventually show up in the numbers.

Within four months, the project was completely turned around and became profitable. What's more, Mushfiq learned the value of recognising contributions. 'It's more than just giving people pay raises,' he explained. 'It's about celebrating success in a more personal way.'

Asked his views on the perception that Australians won't admit that they like public recognition, Mushfiq told us to the contrary:

> I think they love it. It's a good feeling. You don't want people to sit there and go, 'Pick me, pick me, pick me'. But when someone is recognised, they certainly enjoy it. You do have to be careful not to embarrass people sometimes with big public speeches and things like that. I try to do it discreetly and with a little bit of surprise. People are definitely proud of what they've done, and I think that element of surprise is when the manager does recognise them in front of their peers and colleagues.

As Mushfiq learned on this project, exemplary leaders are dedicated to encouraging people by recognising contributions. People who feel taken for granted and unappreciated are not very likely to hang in there when times are tough, or to give their best efforts. When people feel appreciated, they want to do their best. They are given the emotional fuel to make it through challenging times.

Are you Encouraging the Heart?

As you've learned from the examples in this chapter, to Encourage the Heart you must:

- pay attention to what people are doing
- be clear about expectations and standards and hold people accountable
- say 'thank you' to people who have made important contributions
- find ways of personalising any individual recognition
- learn people's names, backgrounds and interests
- keep people posted on the progress they're making towards reaching their goals
- ensure that people are creatively recognised for their contributions to the success of projects
- get personally involved in recognising people and celebrating accomplishments
- bring people together to celebrate the team's accomplishments.

If you want to boost employee engagement, you have to Encourage the Heart of the people you work with. People will not sustain high levels of energy and productivity if they believe that nobody else cares about the hard work they are doing. Ask yourself: about how many times a day do you thank somebody for their contributions to the success of your organisation, to customer service, to safety, to profitability, to product innovation or to other important priorities? Whatever that number is—starting tomorrow, double it.

Of course, you can't make appreciation trivial or insincere and expect any payoffs other than cynicism. Make sure you genuinely care about what's going on. Find ways of getting personally involved. Spend the time necessary to make encouragement personal in other ways by learning about what motivates each of your direct reports and colleagues. And you're not just giving recognition for recognition's sake; you've got to make sure that you link it with the values and vision that serve to focus and guide people's behaviour.

Chapter 7

Exemplary Leadership = High Engagement = Great Results

ONE OF THE FUNDAMENTAL reasons why people don't take the initiative to lead is that too often they believe that leadership is for somebody else, not for them. They think it's beyond their capabilities or capacity. But in talking to people from all walks of life across the globe for more than three decades, we've found that everyone has a story to tell about being a leader, about a time when they were making a difference. Here's just one example of what someone told us about how revealing this reflection can be:

> Growing up, I assumed leaders had certain traits and qualities that I didn't seem to have. I thought there were 'natural' leaders who were born to lead. I thought leadership was the description of what these people did. But when I thought about *my* personal-best

leadership experience, to my surprise I realised I had displayed those same leadership qualities I thought only the 'natural' leaders displayed.

Leadership is clearly within the capacity of every individual. And, just as importantly, we've found that across time, place, position and geography the essential behaviours people were engaging in when at their personal leadership bests are much more similar than they are different. Leadership is local, but it's also universal.

Our research involving leaders in Australia and New Zealand is consistent with these findings. While context certainly makes a difference—whether it is nationality, discipline, industry, socio-economic status or upbringing—the content and process of leadership does not vary much. Indeed, understanding and appreciating the content and process of leadership will enable you to be effective no matter what your circumstances or setting. And the more global the economy and the workforce, the more important it is that you have a common language of leadership—a shared understanding of what leadership is no matter where you are in the world.

In the end, though, being an effective leader is not just about you. It's about how you need to behave in order to get other people to willingly struggle to achieve shared aspirations. What many people come to realise and appreciate is that their personal bests as leaders are really about what they did to make others experience *their* own personal bests. Highly engaged people become leaders.[1] They do whatever is necessary to get the job done—they do what needs to be done through their sweat, imagination and sustained persistence without anyone needing to tell or cajole them to produce. In the highest performing organisations, everyone is a leader.

Leadership engages people and brings out the best in them. And engagement, in turn, drives higher levels of performance and more outstanding accomplishments. This virtuous cycle begins with you becoming and being the best leader you can possibly be. You owe this not just to yourself but also to all of those people who are counting on you to make extraordinary things happen. You can do that by incorporating The Five Practices of Exemplary Leadership into your daily habits and activities.

Model the Way

Clarify values by finding your voice and affirming shared values, and *set the example by aligning actions with shared values.*

Are you clear on what you stand for, and what you stand against? Do you know what your guiding values and leadership philosophy are? Because you can't lead others effectively until you get in tune with who you really are and until you find your authentic voice. As we learned from PwC's Mike McGrath, people willingly follow leaders who are crystal clear on their values and live them with integrity.

We challenge you to spend some time clarifying your personal values and formulating a leadership philosophy. If you had to choose three-to-five specific values that guide your life and decisions, what would they be? If you had to prioritise them, what value would come first? If you had to write your core leadership philosophy in one sentence, what would it say? This really comes down to your 'why' for leadership. Why do you get up every morning and go to work? What drives you? Why do you want to be better? We invite you to spend some time answering those questions and discovering your personal inspiration.

Of course, clarifying your values and philosophy is just the first step. Actually living in accordance with them — as Peter Maher from Macquarie Bank did when he personally spoke to the people whose jobs he was cutting instead of sending someone else in his place — is the hard part. Where have your actions been out of alignment with your values? What can you do to change that?

Your personal values are a starting point, but ultimately you must lead from values shared among the people you lead. Does your organisation (team) have clearly-defined values that govern constructive and destructive behaviours? Have you built consensus around those values? Do you refer back to the values consistently? How well do you set the example in following those values? Do you hold people accountable to them? Remember how Ed Beattie catalysed a turnaround on his project at Chorus, largely as a result of re-instilling clarity, consensus and commitment to the company's core values?

Finally, nothing is more important than your personal example. Values and principles really are just talk unless you as the leader model the behaviours that they define. As Tyrone O'Neill from Optus has shown, if you say you care about customer service, then you had better demonstrate that in your actions. If you say you value honesty and authenticity, then you had better be the most honest, authentic person on your team and in your organisation. If you don't Model the Way and follow through on your promises and commitments, you've lost all credibility, and credibility is the lifeblood of leadership.

Inspire a Shared Vision

Envision the future by imagining exciting and ennobling possibilities, and *enlist others in a common vision by appealing to shared aspirations.*

People will never follow you unless they know where you're leading them and they're inspired by that destination, that result, that future. Managers create efficient systems around the status quo while leaders envision possibilities for doing things better. What possibilities do you envision for your team and organisation? What could the future look like? What impact could you have? How could you make the world a better place? How could you make your organisation grow and what effect would that have on the people you work with?

Once you've found that personal inspiration and vision, you must transform it into a vision that is shared among those you lead. How well are you painting a picture of what the future could look like? Are people really able to grasp, in concrete terms, what the vision looks like—as clearly as Jan Pacas's vision at Hilti of 'Painting Australia Red'? Do your strategies and goals align with the vision?

Is your shared vision focused or scattered? Remember Kirsten O'Doherty's experience at AbbVie? If the vision is not focused, then your energy can very quickly be diffused and rendered ineffective. And even when the vision is focused, you must constantly communicate it to your team. You must keep driving it home until you feel you can't say it one more time. As Louise Baxter showed at Starlight Foundation, everything you say must revolve around the vision. Otherwise, people simply don't take it seriously.

Remember this: People crave being part of something ennobling and inspiring, which is bigger than themselves. People *want* to be enlisted in a vision, a cause. If your team hasn't fully enlisted and engaged yet, it may be because your vision is not clear, concrete and compelling enough, or that you are not appealing to your team's shared aspirations.

Challenge the Process

Search for opportunities by seizing the initiative and looking outward for innovative ways to improve, and *experiment and take risks by constantly generating small wins and learning from experience.*

In today's environment, rapid change is the norm. You can either resist it and be engulfed by it or you can lead it. Leaders don't sit around waiting for things to happen—they make things happen. They are constantly looking for ways of innovating and improving their processes and results. They are *never* content with the status quo. They despise mediocrity. Are you constantly scanning the horizon for new opportunities, as John Studdert did while at Ogilvy Public Relations? Do you study other leaders, industries and organisations for new ideas on how you can improve, as Wendy Lenton at George Weston Foods described? Are you constantly asking, 'Why are we doing it this way?' and 'How can we do it better?', as Cindy Dunham did at Rio Tinto?

Once you identify ways of improving, how bold are you at implementing them? Are you willing to experiment? Are you willing to take risks, as Jodi Williams did at Air New Zealand? Do you create a safe environment in which people can experiment and take risks or do people feel afraid of the consequences of failure?

There's a fine line between being bold and being dumb. Challenging the Process is not about being impulsive, foolhardy or stupid. Your job as leader is to guide the process so that it doesn't get out of hand. Don't bite off more than you can chew—take small bites to generate quick wins, and then build on the momentum of those quick wins, just as Richard Hall did at the University of Sydney Business School. Solicit input and feedback from all team members and genuinely listen to them so that everyone feels safe participating in the process. Encourage people to take risks. When they do and they fail, praise them for taking the initiative, and take time to learn the lessons together so that mistakes aren't repeated. Never waste a failure by not learning from it how to proceed more wisely the next time around.

Enable Others to Act

Foster collaboration by building trust and facilitating relationships, and *strengthen others by increasing self-determination and developing competence.*

Recruiting top talent to your organisation is not enough to drive performance. Even the most highly talented and skilled people will not perform if they don't feel valued, respected and understood. Great skills are worthless in a low-trust environment. Are you creating a high-trust climate? Do you solicit feedback and really listen to it? Do people feel confident that they can share differing opinions without being belittled or shot down? Are you being open and authentic with your team? Do people feel they can approach you? Are you vulnerable with your team or do you put up defensive walls? Interestingly, leaders often feel worried about vulnerability because they feel they will lose credibility by showing weakness. But the truth is that vulnerability makes people trust and respect you more, as Jonathan Moss at Frucor demonstrated.

Ultimately, leadership is about relationships. It's not about you being smarter than everyone else and getting things done by dictating. It's about working with people, not telling them what to do. It's about honesty and communication, as Trish Langridge validated at WaterCare.

Leadership is about bringing out the best in people. This starts by communicating clear expectations and guidance about their individual roles, as Anthony Panuccio at McAfee learned. Do your team members know what's expected of them? Do they know how to perform in their job? Are the guidelines and systems clear? Again, even the most talented people will struggle in an environment where they are not properly trained. Often, leaders will blame people for poor performance and ascribe it to low motivation or mediocrity when the truth is their leaders simply have not provided them with the tools and resources to properly do their job.

People want to do their best. They want to feel competent. They want to feel that they are contributing to the team. Sometimes they don't give their best because they simply lack confidence. As Celia Hodson did with her team at the School of Social Entrepreneurs, you can play a critical role in building people's confidence and therefore their competence. You can treat them with dignity and respect. You can see the best in them, and draw it out through encouraging words and opportunities. You can take quality time to coach and mentor them. When people aren't performing well, your job as a leader isn't to criticise, berate or blame them—it is to encourage, coach and uplift them.

Encourage the Heart

Recognise contributions by showing appreciation for individual excellence, and *celebrate the values and victories by creating a spirit of community.*

Everyone is familiar with the phrase 'back to the grindstone' and the cliché of the dreaded back-to-work Monday. These are common because there is truth to them—people often feel that work is a grind, especially when they are not encouraged. The story is told of an older married couple who went to see a marriage counsellor. The woman tells the counsellor that she doesn't know if her husband still loves her. The man quickly chimes in, 'Of course I love you! I told you that on our marriage night, and I would tell you if anything had changed'.

Of course, leaders know better than the old man in this story. People crave recognition. It's not enough to tell them one time that they're performing well; you have to continually show appreciation for them by recognising their contributions. This can be done through public-recognition celebrations or privately and personally, as Nathalie McNeil at Novartis demonstrated so well. It can be in the form of a formal award or a simple thank-you note. Do the people on your team know you appreciate them? If so, how? What do you do to show them? What can you do better to recognise people for their performance and contribution?

Of course, before you can recognise great accomplishments and behaviours you must first establish standards of performance. Without clear standards of excellence, recognition is done at the whim of the leader. It therefore becomes inauthentic and people suspect favouritism. Keep in mind the practical nature of Encourage the Heart, as explained by Sallie Purser at IBM. This is not simply about niceties; it's about driving performance and getting results.

In your quest to improve your results, never forget to celebrate along the journey. People need to refuel, and one essential way to do this is to bring people together to celebrate accomplishments. Not only does this re-energise people personally, but it also creates a sense of community. People love feeling that they are part of a team, a community of people who care about them and who are striving for the same purpose. When you create a sense of community, as Deven Billimoria at Smartsalary did so well, people become more motivated. They want to do things that benefit the team. In short, they are encouraged to perform at their best.

Excelsior: *The Leadership Challenge*

The mathematics is clear: If A equals B, and B equals C, then A must also equal C. So it is with leadership. If exemplary leadership (A) creates higher levels of engagement (B), and organisations with higher levels of engagement (B) achieve the best results (C), then the best results (most productive and profitable organisations) are a function of exemplary leadership (A). The people who engage most frequently in The Five Practices of Exemplary Leadership create engaged workplaces filled with people holding Positive Workplace Attitudes, willing to make beyond-the-call-of-duty efforts, be innovative and initiate the actions needed to solve problems, address challenges and embrace opportunities.

The question is, will *you* accept the challenge of leadership? Because we know, both from the examples of leaders in this book and from decades of research and experience, that everyone can lead. Few of the leaders we've featured in this book are CEOs. They come from all levels, functions and industries. When you accept *The Leadership Challenge*, you accept and embrace the responsibility to be the CEO in your sphere of influence. You don't wait for others to take action. You see what needs to be done and you step up and do it, tall poppy syndrome or not.

And, make no mistake, leadership is never easy. It's easy to read about leadership. It's easy to attend a leadership training program. It's not easy to actually *apply* what you learn. When we teach seminars on leadership, we finish by asking participants if they heard anything that was too intellectually difficult to understand or grasp. The answer is always no. In other words, great leadership is not reserved for the intellectually brilliant. *The Leadership Challenge* is not intellectual; it's far deeper and more personal.

And so it is with all of us; we know what we need to do, but doing it is a different story. This is why, to really change and improve you must fall deeply in love with the idea of being an exemplary leader. Then and only then will you have the strength and resilience necessary to overcome your resistance and deeply-ingrained habits. Pain and discomfort are inevitable along the leadership journey but, if you stick with it, so are joy and the thrill of accomplishment.

In this book we've given you dozens of things you can do to improve your leadership skills using The Five Practices. Now, what *are* you going to do? What are you going to change in your daily routine? Which new habits will you develop? We challenge you to write down one thing *right now* that you commit to implementing.

Here is one action that I am going to take to be a better leader:

_____

_____

_____

We don't know you personally, but we do know that you can make a difference — and we say this with utmost confidence. The question before you is not, 'Will I make a difference?' — because you will. The real question to consider is, 'Will I make the difference I wanted to make?'

We hope that when you look around and say, 'Something needs to change', or 'Something could be improved or could be better than it is right now', you'll also look in the mirror and see that you are the person who could make that difference.

There's a popular riddle about 12 frogs. It goes like this: If there are 12 frogs sitting on a log at the edge of a pond and five of these 12 frogs decide to jump into the water, how many frogs remain on the log? What's your answer? Seven? Zero? 12? Five?

The correct answer is 12. Twelve frogs remain on the log. Why? Because there is a very big difference between deciding to do something and actually doing it. As you finish reading this book, please keep this riddle in mind.

You've read about how leaders make a difference, and you've learned about The Five Practices of Exemplary Leadership. You've been presented with lots of examples of what leaders in Australia and New Zealand do that makes a difference, and you've been given many suggestions about actions you can take right now without needing any more money, lines of authority or permission. Now that you've decided to do something different in order to be an even better leader, get off the log and into the water!

Endnotes

Introduction

1   The comparisons between Australia and New Zealand and 'other nations around the globe' referred to here and elsewhere in the book are from the Kouzes-Posner normative Leadership Practices Inventory (LPI) database. This database contains responses from more than two million people in 72 countries. The comparison countries referred to are (in alphabetical order) Brazil, Canada, the Caribbean, China, France, Germany, Hong Kong, India, Indonesia, Ireland, Israel, Italy, Japan, Malaysia, Mexico, the Philippines, Saudi Arabia, Singapore, South Africa, South Korea, Spain, Sweden, Switzerland, Taiwan, Thailand, the UK, the US and Vietnam.

2   WS Ramson, *The Australian National Dictionary: A Dictionary of Australianisms on Historical Principles.* New York: Oxford University Press, 1998.

3   L Johansen, *The Penguin Book of Australian Slang: A Dinkum Guide to Oz English* (3rd edition, rev.). Melbourne: Penguin Books, 1996.

4   Egalitarianism in Australia, Convict Creations.Com, viewed 15 August 2014, www.convictcreations.com/culture/egalitarianism.html.

5   Unless otherwise noted, all quotations are from personal interviews. The titles and affiliations of the people may be different today from what they were at the time of their personal-best case study, interview or publication of this book. We expect that many have moved on to other leadership adventures.

6   Egalitarianism in Australia, op. cit.

7   G Aigner & L Skelton, *The Australian Leadership Paradox: What it Takes to Lead in the Lucky Country.* Sydney: Allen & Unwin, 2013, p. 41.

8   ibid. p. 42.

9   It should be noted that the 'tall poppy syndrome' seems to be somewhat diminishing in Australasian culture due to increasing globalisation, the rise of social media and the influx of Generation Y—which in many ways is immune to the phenomenon—into the workforce. Still, it is something for all Australasian leaders to be aware of and sensitive to, particularly as egalitarianism continues to be a core cultural value that looks set to stay.

10 D Ladkin & C Spiller, *Authentic Leadership: Clashes, Convergences, and Coalescences.* Cheltenham, UK: Edward Elgar Publishing Ltd, 2013.

Chapter 1   Exemplary leadership

1   JM Kouzes & BZ Posner, *Turning Adversity into Opportunity.* San Francisco: Jossey-Bass, 2014.

2   JM Kouzes & BZ Posner, *Great Leadership Creates Great Workplaces.* San Francisco: Jossey-Bass, 2013.

3   For more about this research see JM Kouzes & BZ Posner, *The Leadership Challenge: How to Make Extraordinary Things Happen in Organizations* (5th edition). San Francisco: Jossey-Bass, 2012. See also B Posner, 'It's How Leaders Behave That Matters, Not Where They Are From', *Leadership & Organization Development Journal*, vol. 34, no. 6, 2013, pp. 573–87.

4   These results are quite consistent with what Liz Wiseman reports in her book *Multipliers: How the Best Leaders Make Everyone Smarter.* New York: HarperCollins, 2010.

5   For more information about these findings see Kouzes & Posner, 2013, op. cit.

6   LM Brown & BZ Posner, 'Exploring the Relationship Between Learning and Leadership', *Leadership & Organization Development Journal*, vol. 22, no. 6, 2001, pp. 339–51; and BZ Posner, 'Understanding the Learning Tactics of College Students and Their Relationship to Leadership', *Leadership & Organization Development Journal*, vol. 30, no. 4, 2009, pp. 386–95.

7   For more about leadership and learning, see chapter 9 of JM Kouzes & BZ Posner, *The Truth about Leadership: The No-Fads Heart-of-the-Matter Facts You Need to Know.* San Francisco: Jossey-Bass, 2010.

8   This was when Barry was visiting the Graduate School of Management, University of Western Australia, and conducted a week-long management development program jointly sponsored by UWA and the Australian Institute of Management, Western Australia.

9   M Burchell & J Robin, *The Great Workplace: How to Build It, How to Keep It, and Why It Matters.* San Francisco: Jossey-Bass, 2011, pp. 127–8.

10 Research report, *Employee Engagement in a VUCA World: a Review of Current Research and Its Implications*, Conference Board, New York, 2011.

11 Towers Watson, '2012 Global Workforce Study—Australia', Australian and New Zealand Normative Database, 2013.

12 Aon Hewitt, Best Employers Australia and New Zealand Presentation, 2014.

13 Gallup, 'State of the Global Workplace: Employee Engagement Insights for Business Leaders Worldwide', viewed 17 August 2014, www.gallup.com/strategicconsulting/164735/state-global-workplace.aspxfor.

14   R Beck & J Harter, 'Why Great Managers are So Rare', *Gallup Business Journal*, viewed 25 March 2014, www.businessjournal.gallup.com/content/167975/why-great-managers-rare.aspx.
15   The nine factors (or variables) are the respondent's age, gender, educational level, functional area, where they are in their organisation's hierarchy, their organisation's size (number of employees), how long they've been with the company, the industry in which they work and which country they are from.
16   Abstracts of these studies can be found at www.theleadershipchallenge.com/research.
17   R Roi, *Leadership Practices, Corporate Culture, and Company Financial Performance*. Palo Alto: Crawford & Associates, 2006.

Chapter 2   Model the Way

1   JM Kouzes and BZ Posner, 'To Lead, Create a Shared Vision', *Harvard Business Review*, January–February 2009, pp. 20–1.
2   Towers Watson, '2012 Global Workforce Study—Australia', Australian and New Zealand Normative Database, 2013, pp. 11–12.
3   T Simons, *The Integrity Dividend*. San Francisco: Jossey-Bass, 2008.
4   ibid.
5   For more on this, see JM Kouzes & BZ Posner, *Credibility: How Leaders Gain and Lose It, Why People Demand It* (2nd edition). San Francisco: Jossey Bass, 2012.
6   G Aigner & L Skelton, *The Australian Leadership Paradox: What it Takes to Lead in the Lucky Country*. Sydney: Allen & Unwin, 2013, p. 37.
7   ibid. p. 43.

Chapter 3   Inspire a Shared Vision

1   Towers Watson, '2012 Global Workforce Study—Australia', Australian and New Zealand Normative Database, 2013.
2   Kenexa, 'Empower Your People: It's All Part of a Smarter Workforce', 2013.

Chapter 4   Challenge the Process

1   G Aigner & L Skelton, *The Australian Leadership Paradox: What it Takes to Lead in the Lucky Country*. Sydney: Allen & Unwin, 2013, p. 56.
2   Towers Watson, '2012 Global Workforce Study—Australia', Australian and New Zealand Normative Database, 2013.

Chapter 5   Enable Others to Act

1   Innovation Survey, PricewaterhouseCoopers, London, 1999, p. 3. See also PS Shockley-Zalabak, S Morreale & M Hackman, *Building the High-Trust Organization: Strategies for Supporting Five Key Dimensions of Trust*. San Francisco: Jossey-Bass, 2010.

Chapter 6   Encourage the Heart

1   Towers Watson, '2012 Global Workforce Study—Australia', Australian and New Zealand Normative Database, 2013.

2   For more on this topic, see JM Kouzes & BZ Posner, *Encouraging the Heart: A Leader's Guide to Rewarding and Recognizing Others*. San Francisco: Jossey-Bass, 1999.

Chapter 7   Exemplary Leadership = High Engagement = Great Results

1   For more about this, see S Edinger & L Sain, *The Hidden Leader*. New York: AMACOM, 2015.

Acknowledgements

It's publishing tradition to call the section at the end of a book, in which authors thank everyone, 'Acknowledgements'. However, *acknowledgement* is too weak a word to express the emotions we feel as we reflect back on all those who were part of this undertaking. *Gratitude* is so much better. It captures the spirit of how thankful and appreciative we are to the very talented, hardworking and uplifting people with whom we collaborated on this project. They encouraged, supported, coached, enlightened and enabled us so that we could get to this place. First on the list are the many people we interviewed who contributed to our understanding of leadership in Australia and New Zealand. Many are mentioned by name in the text and others are not, but we wholeheartedly thank each and every one of these individuals for sharing their experiences and insights:

Anne Adamson	Dave Adler	Geoff Aigner	Steve Allman
Scott Archibald	Rachel Argaman	Henning Arndt	Guy Bader
Shelley Ballard	Louise Baxter	Ed Beattie	Mary Bennet
Matt Benwell	Belinda Betts	Toby Bicknell	Deven Billimoria
Brian Bissaker	Vicki Brady	Vivien Bridgewater	Lesley Brown
Peter Butler	Tania Candy	Sid Chandra	Mai Chen
Gary Cheng	Peter Chrystal	Ramsay Chu	Giuseppe Cirillo
Megan Clark	Lisa Cronin	Steve Dahllof	Tony Davey
Cameron Davidson	Susan Davidson	Carol Douglas	Cindy Dunham
James Dunne	Michael Ellis	Steve Faruggia	Andrew Fox
Maurice Furlong	Heidi George	Steve Gleadell	Lawrence Goldstone
David Grant	Zoe Grose	Nis Hakea	Adam Hall
Richard Hall	Scott Hastie	Susan Henry	Stephen Hickey
Stephen Hill	Richard Hirst	Celia Hodson	Amanda Hutton
Eleni Isaias	Judy Jaeger	Aasif Javed	Arvin Jayabalan
Mick Jenner	Emma Jenson	Sam Kelleher	Roseline Klein
Matt Kulmar	Ben Lancken	Trish Langridge	Nick Leach
Houda Lebbos	Wendy Lenton	Zrinka Lovrencic	Emma Lowe
Maria Lyons	John Maasland	Peter Maher	Cheryl Maley
Emma Martin	Lucas Masters	Marina Matthews	Tanya Matthewson

ACKNOWLEDGEMENTS

Shaun McCarthy	Derek McCormack	Sally McGeoch	Mike McGrath
Fellicity McMahon	Nathalie McNeil	Charles Moore	Lou Morrissey
Jonathon Moss	Suvendu Mukherjee	Nick Nairn	Ken Neate
Oona Nielssen	Louise Norris	Kirsten O'Doherty	Tyrone O'Neill
Jan Pacas	Anthony Panuccio	Trent Paterson	Mike Peppou
Fabrizio Perilli	Michelle Pombart	Sallie Purser	Mushfiq Rahman
Andrew Reeves	Severino Refuerzo	Rhonda Richardson	Tony Ritchie
Rebecca Rock	John Rose	James Rutherford	Carol Saab
Dean Sappey	Danny Shepherd	Jason Smith	Chris Sozou
Chellie Spiller	Rodger Spiller	Andrew Stammer	John Studdert
Carlo Sutherland	Craig Swanger	Jim Swanson	Doug Taylor
Andrew Thomas	Mike Tod	Thien Tran	Sheridan Tranter
Nick Wailes	David Wallace	Kristine Walsh	Kellie Warta
Geoff Watson	Andrew Weeks	Lynn Wheeler	John Wilhelm
Danielle Williams	Jessie Williams	Jodi Williams	

A special shout out goes to Rodger Spiller, our friend and colleague from WorkSmart New Zealand, who was especially generous with his time, effort and insights. Similarly generous were colleagues from Aon Hewitt, Towers Watson and Great Place to Work who shared their research reports and perspectives about leadership challenges in Australia and New Zealand.

We want to thank Marisa Kelley, Product Manager for Workplace Learning Solutions and *The Leadership Challenge*, for her continuing support in expanding the global reach of *The Leadership Challenge* brand. We are grateful to Kristen Hammond, Senior Commissioning Editor with Wiley (Melbourne), who guided this manuscript from the editorial process through to production. Marisa and Kristen were our champions inside Wiley, and without them the book wouldn't have made it past the pitch. Thank you also to Ingrid Bond, Publishing Coordinator, and Alice Berry, Senior Editor, at Wiley Melbourne, for their superb support and craftsmanship throughout the editorial and publishing cycle.

A high, high-five, and one down low, to Leslie Stephen, our developmental editor, who continues to help us write clearly and concisely. We've worked with Leslie on several manuscripts, and she has helped to transform concepts, cases and data into more readable prose. Another huge shout out goes to Sandra Balonyi, who carefully helped us smooth out the rough edges in the manuscript and prepare the manuscript for Australasian publication.

Others at Wiley who have made a difference in making this book a reality are Lisa Shannon, Erik Thrasher, and CJ Hwu. After 30 years of working with one publisher we remain always grateful for the expertise and generosity of the best team in the business.

From Michael, a special word of thanks goes to Rachel Laws and to the team at WorkSmart. Your efforts in helping earmark exceptional leaders, keeping track of schedules and revisions, proofreading and attending to many other back-office details are deeply appreciated.

Whenever we write we know that we are stealing precious time from our awesome spouses: time to think, and write, and edit, and revise, and think, and write, and edit, and revise—a process that may seem to them to go on forever. And they are always with us, sometimes urging us on, sometimes telling us it's time to take a break and very often adding exceptional ideas from their own professional experiences that make the work much better. We express our gratitude to Tae Moon Kouzes, Jackie Schmidt-Posner and Natasha Pilgrim for their love, encouragement, sacrifices and graciousness. Without them we could not make the contributions that we aspire to make.

About the authors

Jim Kouzes and **Barry Posner** have been working together for more than 30 years, studying leaders, researching leadership, conducting leadership-development seminars and serving as leaders themselves in various capacities. They are co-authors of the award-winning, best-selling book *The Leadership Challenge*, now in its fifth edition. Since its first edition in 1987, *The Leadership Challenge* has sold more than 2 million copies worldwide and is available in 21 languages. It has won numerous awards, including the Critics' Choice Award from the nation's book review editors and the James A Hamilton Hospital Administrators' Book of the Year Award; it has been named a Best Business Book of the Year (2012) by *Fast Company*, and was selected as one of the top-10 books on leadership in Covert & Sattersten's *The 100 Best Business Books of All Time*.

Jim and Barry have co-authored more than a dozen other award-winning leadership books, including *Turning Adversity into Opportunity; Finding the Courage to Lead; Great Leadership Creates Great Workplaces; Making Extraordinary Things Happen in*

Asia: Applying The Five Practices of Exemplary Leadership®; Credibility: How Leaders Gain and Lose It, Why People Demand It; The Truth About Leadership: The No-Fads, Heart-of-the-Matter Facts You Need to Know; A Leader's Legacy; Encouraging the Heart: A Leader's Guide to Rewarding and Recognizing Others; The Student Leadership Challenge; and *Academic Administrator's Guide to Exemplary Leadership.*

They also developed the highly acclaimed Leadership Practices Inventory (LPI), a 360-degree questionnaire for assessing leadership behaviour, which is one of the most widely used leadership assessment instruments in the world. More than 700 research studies, doctoral dissertations and academic papers have been based on their The Five Practices of Exemplary Leadership® model.

Among the honours and awards that Jim and Barry have received is the American Society for Training and Development's highest award for their Distinguished Contribution to Workplace Learning and Performance. They have been named Management/Leadership Educators of the Year by the International Management Council; ranked by *Leadership Excellence* magazine in the top 20 on its list of the Top 100 Thought Leaders; named among the 50 Top Coaches in the US (according to *Coaching for Leadership*); ranked as Top 100 Thought Leaders in Trustworthy Business Behavior by Trust Across America; and listed among *HR* magazine's Most Influential International Thinkers.

Jim and Barry are frequent keynote speakers, and each has conducted leadership-development programs for hundreds of organisations, including Alberta Health Services, ANZ, Apple, Applied Materials, ARCO, AT&T, Australian Institute of Management, Australia Post, Bank of America, Bose, Charles Schwab, Chevron, Cisco Systems, Clorox, Community Leadership Association, Conference Board of Canada, Consumers Energy, Deloitte Touche, Dorothy Wylie Nursing and Health Leaders

ABOUT THE AUTHORS

Institute, Dow Chemical, Egon Zehnder International, Federal Express, Genentech, Google, Gymboree, HP, IBM, Jobs DR-Singapore, Johnson & Johnson, Kaiser Foundation Health Plans and Hospitals, Korean Management Association, Intel, Itau Unibanco, LL Bean, Lawrence Livermore National Labs, Lucile Packard Children's Hospital, Merck, Monsanto, Motorola, NetApp, Northrop Grumman, Novartis, Oakwood Temporary Housing, Oracle, Petronas, Pixar, Roche Bioscience, Telstra, Siemens, Silicon Valley Bank, Stanford University, 3M, TIAA-CREF, Toyota, United Way, USAA, Verizon, VISA, Vodafone, Walt Disney Company, Western Mining Corporation and Westpac. They have lectured at more than 60 college and university campuses.

* * *

Jim Kouzes is the Dean's Executive Fellow of Leadership, Leavey School of Business at Santa Clara University. He lectures on

leadership around the world to corporations, governments and nonprofits. He is a highly regarded leadership scholar and an experienced executive; the *Wall Street Journal* cited him as one of the 12 best executive educators in the US. In 2010, Jim received the Thought Leadership Award from the Instructional

Systems Association, the most prestigious award given by the trade association of training and development industry providers. He was listed as one of *HR* magazine's Most Influential International Thinkers for 2010 through 2012, named one of the 2010 through 2014 Top 100 Thought Leaders in Trustworthy Business Behavior by Trust Across America, and ranked by *Leadership Excellence* magazine as number 16 on its list of the Top 100 Thought Leaders. In 2006, Jim was presented with the Golden Gavel, the highest honour awarded by Toastmasters International. Jim served as president, CEO and chairman of the Tom Peters Company from 1988 through 2000, and prior to that led the Executive Development Center at Santa Clara University (1981–88). Jim founded the Joint Center for Human Services Development at San Jose State University (1972–80) and was on the staff of the School of Social Work, University of Texas. His career in training and development began in 1969 when he conducted seminars for Community Action Agency staff and volunteers in the war on poverty. Following graduation from Michigan State University (BA degree with honours in political science), he served as a Peace Corps volunteer (1967–69). Jim can be reached at jim@kouzes.com.

* * *

Barry Posner is the Accolti Endowed Professor of Leadership at the Leavey School of Business, Santa Clara University, where he

served as dean of the school for 12 years (1997–2009). He has been a distinguished visiting professor at Hong Kong University of Science and Technology, Sabanci University (Istanbul) and the University of Western Australia. At Santa Clara he received the President's Distinguished Faculty Award, the School's Extraordinary Faculty Award, and several other teaching and academic honours. Barry has been named one of his nation's top management and leadership educators by the International Management Council; recognised as one of the Top 50 leadership coaches in America and one of the Top 100 Thought Leaders in Trustworthy Business Behavior; ranked among the Most Influential HR thinkers in the world; and listed among the Top Leadership and Management Experts in the world by *Inc.* magazine. An internationally renowned scholar and educator, Barry is author or co-author of more than 100 research and practitioner-focused articles. He currently serves on the editorial boards for the *Leadership & Organizational Development Journal* and the *International Journal of Servant-Leadership*. In 2011, he received the Outstanding Scholar Award for Career Achievement from the *Journal of Management Inquiry*.

Barry received his BA with honours in political science from the University of California, Santa Barbara; his MA in public administration from The Ohio State University; and his PhD in organisational behaviour and administrative theory from the University of Massachusetts, Amherst. Having consulted with a wide variety of public and private sector organisations around the globe, Barry also works at a strategic level with a number of community-based and professional organisations, currently sitting on the board of directors of EMQ FamiliesFirst and the Global Women's Leadership Network. He has served previously on the boards of the American Institute of Architects (AIA), Big Brothers/ Big Sisters of Santa Clara County, Center for Excellence in Nonprofits, Junior Achievement of Silicon Valley and Monterey Bay, Public Allies, San Jose Repertory Theater, Sigma Phi Epsilon Fraternity, and both publicly traded and start-up companies. Barry can be reached at bposner@scu.edu.

*   *   *

Michael Bunting has been working with Jim and Barry and *The Leadership Challenge* community for more than six years. He has

 worked in the field of leadership development, organisational development, leadership research and leadership program design and development for more than 15 years. He is the founder and managing director of WorkSmart, based in Sydney, Australia. He has an honours degree in Business

Administration from the University of Kwazulu Natal and received a postgraduate diploma in psychotherapy from Sophia College in Western Australia. Michael has lived and worked in three different countries and launched two other successful businesses in addition to WorkSmart. He is also currently a guest lecturer in the University of Sydney's award-winning Executive MBA program, teaching as part of their leadership development module.

Michael and his team typically work with organisations over the long term and specialise in developing world-class leaders and leadership cultures that make a measurable difference to engagement, talent attraction and retention, and overall profitability. Over the past decade Michael and his colleagues have worked with many well-known organisations in Australia and New Zealand including Abbott Australasia, AbbVie Australasia, Broadcast Australia, Broad Construction Services, BOS International, Cantarella Brothers, Capital Finance, Centrelink, Commonwealth Bank, Elanco Australia New Zealand, Eli Lilly Australia, Greens General Foods, Hilti Australia, Hutchison Telecoms, iNova Pharmaceuticals, Leighton Contractors, Macquarie Bank, Mizuho Bank, Novartis Australia, Nutrimetics Australia New Zealand, Newcastle City Council, Ogilvy Worldwide PR, PwC Australia and New Zealand, SAI Global and TFE Hotels. Contact Michael at mbunting@worksmart.net.au.

Suggested reading

Here's a varied list of books you should take a look at if you want to continue developing your leadership capabilities.

General Leadership

G Aigner & L Skelton, *The Australian Leadership Paradox: What it Takes to Lead in the Lucky Country*. Sydney: Allen & Unwin, 2013.

J Badaracco, *Defining Moments: When Managers Must Choose Between Right and Right*. Boston, Harvard Business Press, 1997.

W Bennis, *On Becoming a Leader*. Reading, Massachusetts: Perseus, 1994.

LG Bolman & TE Deal, *How Great Leaders Think: The Art Of* Reframing. San Francisco: Jossey-Bass, 2014.

J MacGregor Burns, *Leadership*. New York: HarperCollins, 1978.

J Collins, *Good to Great: Why Some Companies Make the Leap and Others Don't*. New York: HarperCollins, 2001.

J Collins & J Porras, *Built to Last: Successful Habits of Visionary Companies*. New York: HarperBusiness, 1994.

C Conley, *Peak: How Great Companies Get Their Mojo from Maslow*. San Francisco: Jossey-Bass, 2007.

H Gardner, *Leading Minds: An Anatomy of Leadership*. New York: Basic Books, 1995.

J Gardner, *On Leadership*. New York: The Free Press, 1990.

B George, *Authentic Leadership: Rediscovering the Secrets to Creating Lasting Value*. San Francisco: Jossey-Bass, 2004.

JM Kouzes & BZ Posner, *The Truth About Leadership: The No-Fads, Heart-of-the-Matter Facts You Should Know*. San Francisco: Jossey-Bass, 2010.

JM Kouzes & BZ Posner, *A Leader's Legacy*. San Francisco: Jossey-Bass, 2006.

JM Kouzes & BZ Posner, *The Leadership Challenge* (5th edition). San Francisco: Jossey-Bass, 2012.

J Pfeffer & R Sutton. *Hard Facts, Dangerous Half-Truths & Total Nonsense: Profiting from Evidence-Based Management*. Boston: Harvard Business School Press, 2006.

RE Quinn, *Building the Bridge as You Walk on It*. Jossey-Bass, 2004.

S Sandberg, *Lean In: Women, Work, and the Will to Lead*. New York: Knopf, 2013.

EH Schein, *Organizational Culture and Leadership* (4th edition). San Francisco: Jossey-Bass, 2010.

Model the Way

DM Armstrong, *Managing by Storying Around: A New Method of Leadership*. New York: Doubleday, 1992.

JA Autry, *The Servant Leader: How to Build a Creative Team, Develop Great Morale & Improve Bottom-Line Performance*. New York: Three Rivers Press, 2004.

W Bennis, D Goleman & J O'Toole, *Transparency: How Leaders Create a Culture of Candor*. San Francisco: Jossey-Bass, 2008.

P Bronson, *What Should I Do with My Life? The True Story of People Who Answered the Ultimate Question*. New York: Random House, 2001.

B Brown, *Daring Greatly: How the Courage to Be Vulnerable Transforms the Way We Live, Love, Parent, and Lead*. New York: Gotham, 2012.

SR Covey, *The Seven Habits of Highly Effective People*. New York: Simon & Schuster Inc., 1989.

S Denning, *The Secret Language of Leadership: How Leaders Inspire Action Through Narrative*. San Francisco: Jossey-Bass, 2007.

M De Pree, *Leadership Is an Art*. New York: Doubleday, 1989.

A Deutschman, *Walk the Talk: The #1 Rule for Real Leaders*. New York: Portfolio, 2009.

B George with P Sims, *True North: Discover Your Authentic Leadership*. San Francisco: Jossey-Bass, 2007.

M Goldsmith, *MOJO: How to Get It, How to Keep It, How to Get It Back If You Lose It*. New York: Hyperion, 2010.

M Goldsmith, *What Got You Here Won't Get You There: How Successful People Become Even More Successful*. New York: Hyperion, 2007.

RK Greenleaf, *Servant Leadership: A Journey Into Legitimate Power and Greatness* (25th anniversary edition). Mahwah, NJ: Paulist Press, 2002.

JM Kouzes & BZ Posner, *Credibility: How Leaders Gain and Lose It, Why People Demand It*. San Francisco: Jossey-Bass, 2003.

HMJ Kraemer, Jr., *From Values to Action: The Four Principles of Values-Based Leadership*. San Francisco: Jossey-Bass, 2011.

D Ladkin & C Spiller. *Authentic Leadership: Clashes, Convergences, and Coalescences*. Edward Elgar Publishing, 2013.

EJ Langer, *Mindfulness*. Reading, Massachusetts.: Addison-Wesley, 1989.

DH Maister, *Practice What You Preach: What Managers Must Do to Create a High Achievement Culture.* New York: Free Press, 2001.

PJ Palmer, *Let Your Life Speak: Listening to the Voice of Vocation.* San Francisco: Jossey-Bass, 2000.

T Pearce, *Leading Out Loud: The Authentic Speaker, The Credible Leader.* San Francisco: Jossey-Bass, 1995.

A Rhoads, *Build on Values: Creating an Enviable Culture That Outperforms the Competition.* San Francisco: Jossey-Bass, 2011.

T Simons, *The Integrity Dividend: Leading by the Power of Your Word.* San Francisco: Jossey-Bass, 2008.

C Wortmann, *What's Your Story? Using Stories to Ignite Performance and Be More Successful.* Chicago: Kaplan Publishing, 2006.

Inspire a Shared Vision

M Burchell & Jennifer Robin, *The Great Workplace: How to Build It, How to Keep It, and Why It Matters.* San Francisco: Jossey-Bass, 2011.

E Cornish, *Futuring: The Exploration of the Future.* Bethesda, Maryland: The World Future Society, 2005.

B Clarke & R Crossland, *The Leaders Voice: How Your Communication Can Inspire Action and Get Results!* New York: Select Books, 2002.

C Gallo, *Talk Like TED: The 9 Public-Speaking Secrets of the World's Top Minds.* New York: St. Martin's Press, 2014.

J Geary, *I Is an Other: The Secret Life of Metaphor and How It Shapes the Way We See the World.* New York: Harper, 2012.

B Linda Halpren & K Lubar, *Leadership Presence: Dramatic Techniques to Reach Out, Motivate, and Inspire.* New York: Gotham Books, 2003.

G Hamel, *Leading the Revolution,* Boston: Harvard Business School Press, 2000.

C Heath & D Heath, *Made to Stick: Why Some Ideas Survive and Others Die.* New York: Random House, 2007.

J James, *Thinking in the Future Tense: Leadership Skills for the New Age.* New York: Simon & Schuster, 1996.

R Johansen, *Get There Early: Sensing the Future to Compete in the Present.* San Francisco: Berrett-Koehler, 2007.

R Johansen, *Leaders Make the Future: The New Leadership Skills for an Uncertain World.* San Francisco: Berrett-Koehler, 2009.

JM Kouzes and BZ Posner, *A Leader's Legacy.* San Francisco: Jossey-Bass, 2006.

R Leider, *The Power of Purpose: Find Meaning, Live Longer, Better.* San Francisco: Berrett-Koehler, 2010.

R Maxwell & R Dickman, *The Elements of Persuasion: Use Storytelling to Pitch Better Ideas, Sell Faster, & Win More Business.* New York: HarperCollins, 2007.

DH Pink, *Drive: The Surprising Truth about What Motivates Us.* New York: Riverhead Books, 2009.

J Naisbitt, *Mindset: Eleven Ways to Change the Way You See-and Create-the Future.* New York: HarperCollins, 2006.

B Nanus, *Visionary Leadership*. San Francisco: Jossey-Bass, 1992.

S Sinek, *Start With Why: How Great Leaders Inspire Everyone to Take Action*. New York: Portfolio, 2011.

RS Sisodia, DB Wolfe & JN Sheth, *Firms of Endearment: How World-Class Companies Profit from Passion and Purpose*. Upper Saddle River, NJ: Wharton School Publishing, 2007.

RM Spence, Jr. with H Rushing, *It's Not What You Sell, It's What You Stand For: Why Every Extraordinary Business Is Driven by Purpose*. New York: Portfolio, 2010.

B Sterling, *Tomorrow Now: Envisioning the Next Fifty Years*. New York: Random House, 2003.

D Ulrich & W Ulrich, *The Why of Work: How Great Leaders Build Abundant Organizations that Win*. New York: McGraw Hill, 2010.

Challenge the Process

T Amabile & S Kramer, *The Progress Principle: Using Small Wins to Ignite Joy*. Boston: Harvard Business Review Press, 2011.

D Ariely, *Predictably Irrational: The Hidden Forces that Shape Our Decisions (Revised and Expanded)*. New York: HarperCollins, 2009.

MH Bazerman, *The Power of Noticing: What the Best Leaders See*. New York: Simon & Schuster, 2014.

A Blum, *Annapurna: A Woman's Place* (20th anniversary edition). San Francisco: Sierra Club Books, 1998.

E Catmull & A Wallace, *Creativity, Inc.: Overcoming the Unseen Forces That Stand in the Way of True Inspiration*. New York: Random House, 2014.

M Csikszentmihalyi, *Flow: The Psychology of Optimal Engagement in Life*. New York: Harper Perennial Modern Classics, 2008.

R Farson & R Keyes, *Whoever Makes the Most Mistakes Wins: The Paradox of Innovation*. New York: The Free Press, 2002.

R Foster & S Kaplan, *Creative Destruction: Why Companies that Are Built to Last Underperform the Market—and How to Successfully Transform Them*. New York: Currency, 2001.

EH Friedman, *A Failure of Nerve: Leadership in the Age of the Quick Fix*. New York: Seabury Books, 2007.

B George, *Seven Lessons for Leading in Crisis*. San Francisco: Jossey-Bass, 2009.

M Gladwell, *Blink: The Power of Thinking Without Thinking*. New York: Little, Brown, 2005.

G Hamel with B Breen, *The Future of Management*. Boston: Harvard Business School Press, 2007.

R Heifitz & M Linsky, *Leadership on the Line: Staying Alive through the Dangers of Leading*. Boston: Harvard Business School Press, 2002.

S Johnson, *Where Good Ideas Come From: The Natural History of Innovation*. New York: Riverhead, 2010.

R Moss Kanter, *Confidence: How Winning Streaks & Losing Streaks Begin & End*. New York: Three Rivers Press, 2007.

T Kelley with J Littman, *The Art of Innovation: Lessons in Creativity from IDEO, America's Leading Design Firm.* New York: Currency Doubleday, 2005.

G Klein, *Intuition at Work: Why Developing Your Gut Instincts Will Make You Better at What You Do.* New York: Currency Doubleday, 2003.

TA Kolditz, *In Extremis Leadership: Leading As If Your Life Depended On It.* San Francisco: Jossey-Bass, 2007.

RJ Kriegel & L Patler, *If It Ain't Broke, Break It!* New York: Warner Books, 1991.

S Maddi & D Khoshaba, *Resilience at Work: How to Succeed No Matter What Life Throws at You.* New York: AMACOM, 2005.

R Pausch with J Zaslow, *The Last Lecture.* New York: Hyperion, 2008.

J Robin & M Burchell, *No Excuses: How You Can Turn Any Workplace Into a Great One.* San Francisco: Jossey-Bass, 2013.

KW Thomas, *Intrinsic Motivation at Work: What Really Drives Employee Engagement.* San Francisco: Berrett-Koehler, 2009.

M Useem, *The Go Point: When It's Time to Decide—Knowing What to Do and When to Do It.* New York: Three Rivers Press, 2006.

Enable Others to Act

M Abrashoff, *It's Your Ship: Management Techniques from the Best Damn Ship in the Navy.* New York: Warner, 2002.

W Bennis & P Ward Biederman, *Organizing Genius: The Secrets of Creative Collaboration.* Reading, Massachusetts: Addison-Wesley, 1998.

K Blanchard, J Carlos & A Randolph, *The Three Keys to Empowerment.* San Francisco: Berrett-Koehler, 1999.

H Bracey, *Building Trust: How to Get! How to Keep It!* Taylorsville, GA: HR Artworks, 2002.

P Block, *The Empowered Manager: Positive Political Skills at Work.* San Francisco: Jossey-Bass, 1987.

L Branham, *The Seven Hidden Reasons Employees Leave: How to Recognize the Subtle Signs and Act Before It's Too Late.* New York: AMACOM, 2005.

D Brooks, *The Social Animal: Hidden Sources of Love, Character, and Achievement.* New York: Random House, 2011.

M Buckingham & C Coffman, *First, Break all the Rules: What the World's Greatest Managers Do Differently.* New York: Simon & Schuster, 1999.

C Cherniss & D Goleman, eds, *The Emotionally Intelligent Workplace: How to Select for, Measure, and Improve Emotional Intelligence in Individuals, Groups, and Organizations.* San Francisco: Jossey-Bass, 2001.

RB Cialdini, *Influence: How and Why People Agree to Things.* New York: Marrow, 1984.

SR Covey with RR Merrill, *The Speed of Trust: The One Thing That Changes Everything.* New York: Free Press, 2008.

D DeSteno, *The Truth About Trust: How It Determines Success in Life, Love, Learning, and More.* New York: Hudson Street Press, 2014.

S Edinger & L Sain, *The Hidden Leader.* New York: AMACOM, 2015.

142

EXTRAORDINARY LEADERSHIP IN AUSTRALIA & NEW ZEALAND

D Goleman, *Emotional Intelligence: Why It Can Matter More than IQ* (10th anniversary edition). New York: Bantam, 2006.

D Goleman, Richard Boyatzis & Annie McKee, *Primal Leadership: Realizing the Power of Emotional Intelligence*. Boston: Harvard Business School Press, 2004.

M Gladwell, *The Tipping Point: How Little Things Make a Big Difference*. Boston, MA: Little, Brown and Company, 2002.

A Grant, *Give and Take: Why Helping Others Drives Our Success*. New York: Penguin Books, 2014.

RF Hurley, *The Decision to Trust: How Leaders Create High-Trust Organizations*. San Francisco: Jossey-Bass, 2012.

J Katzenbach & Z Kahn, *Leading Outside the Lines: How to Mobilize the Informal Organization, Energize Your Team and Get Better Results*. San Francisco: Jossey-Bass, 2010.

P Lencioni, *The Five Dysfunctions of a Team: A Field Guide for Leaders, Managers, and Facilitators*. San Francisco: Jossey-Bass, 2005.

C Li, *Open Leadership: How Social Technology Can Transform the Way You Lead*. San Francisco: Jossey-Bass, 2010.

D Marquet, *Turn the Ship Around: A True Story of Turning Followers Into Leaders*. Portfolio, 2013.

K Patterson, J Grenny, R McMillan & A Switzler, *Crucial Conversations: Tools for Talking When Stakes Are High*. New York: McGraw-Hill, 2002.

T Rath, *Vital Friends: The People You Can't Afford to Live Without*. New York: Gallup Press, 2006.

D Reina and M Reina, *Trust & Betrayal in the Workplace: Building Effective Relationships in Your Organization*. San Francisco: Berrett-Koehler, 2006.

D Reina & M Reina, *Rebuilding Trust in the Workplace: Seven Steps to Renew Confidence, Commitment, and Energy*. San Francisco: Berrett-Koehler, 2010.

E Rosen, *The Culture of Collaboration: Maximizing Time, Talent and Tools to Create Value in a Global Economy*. San Francisco: Red Ape Publishing, 2007.

T Sanders, *The Likeability Factor: How to Boost Your L-Factor and Achieve Your Life's Dreams*. New York: HaperCollins, 2006.

PS Shockley-Zalabak, S Morreale & M Hackman, *Building the High Trust Organization: Strategies for Supporting Five Key Dimensions of Trust*. San Francisco: Jossey-Bass, 2010.

J Stack & B Burlingham, *A Stake in the Outcome: Building a Culture of Ownership for the Long-Term Success of Your Business*. New York: Currency Doubleday, 2002.

J Surowiecki, *The Wisdom of Crowds: Why the Many Are Smarter Than the Few and How Collective Wisdom Shapes Business, Economies, Societies and Nations*. New York: Anchor Books, 2005.

KW Thomas, *Intrinsic Motivation: What Really Drives Employee Engagement* (2nd edition). San Francisco: Berrett-Koehler, 2009.

L Wiseman, *Multipliers: How the Best Leaders Make Everyone Smarter*. New York: HarperCollins, 2010.

Encourage the Heart

S Achor, *The Happiness Advantage: The Seven Principles of Positive Psychology That Fuel Success and Performance at Work*. New York: Crown Books, 2010.

R Boyatzis & A McKee, *Resonant Leadership*. Boston: Harvard Business School Press, 2005.

K Blanchard & S Bowles, *Gung Ho! Turn on the People in Any Organization*. New York: William Morrow, 1997.

J Hope Bryant, *Love Leadership: The New Way to Lead in a Fear-Based World*. San Francisco: Jossey-Bass, 2009.

KS Cameron, *Positive Leadership: Strategies for Extraordinary Performance*. San Francisco: Berrett-Koehler, 2008.

GD Chapman & PE White, *The 5 Languages of Appreciation in the Workplace: Empowering Organizations by Encouraging People*. Northfield Publishing, 2012.

T Deal & MK Deal, *Corporate Celebrations: Play, Purpose, and Profit at Work*. San Francisco: Berrett-Koehler, 1998.

BL Fredrickson, *Positivity: Groundbreaking Research Reveals How to Embrace the Hidden Strengths of Positive Emotions, Overcome Negativity, and Thrive*. New York: Crown Publishers, 2009.

A Gostick & S Christopher, *The Levity Effect: Why It Pays to Lighten Up*. Hoboken, NJ: John Wiley & Sons, 2008.

A Gostick & C Elton, *The Carrot Principle: How the Best Managers Use Recognition to Engage Their People, Retain Talent, and Accelerate Performance* (updated and expanded). New York: Free Press, 2009.

HG Halvorson, *Succeed: How We Can Reach Our Goals*. New York: Hudson Street Press, 2010.

D Hemsath & L Yerkes, *301 Ways to Have Fun at Work*. San Francisco: Berrett-Koehler, 1997.

B Kaye & S Jordan-Evans, *Love 'Em or Lose 'Em: Getting Good People to Stay* (4th edition). San Francisco: Berrett-Koehler, 2008.

A Kohn, *Punished by Rewards: The Trouble with Gold Stars, Incentive Plans, A's, Praise and Other Bribes*. New York: Houghton Mifflin, 1999.

JM Kouzes & BZ Posner, *Encouraging the Heart: A Leader's Guide to Rewarding and Recognizing Others*. San Francisco: Jossey-Bass, 2003.

B Nelson, *1001 Ways to Reward Employees*. New York: Workman, 2005.

T Rath & D Clifton, D.O. *How Full Is Your Bucket: Positive Strategies for Work and Life*. New York: Gallup Press, 2004.

T Rath & J Harter, *Well Being: The Five Essential Elements*. New York: Gallup Press, 2010.

LA Yerkes, *Fun Works: Creating Places Where People Love to Work* (2nd edition). Berrett-Koehler, 2007.

Leadership Development

J Conger & RE Riggio, eds. *The Practice of Leadership: Developing the Next Generation of Leaders.* San Francisco: Jossey Bass, 2006

G Colvin, *Talent Is Overrated: What Really Separates World-Class Performers from Everybody Else.* New York: Portfolio, 2008.

D Coyle, *The Talent Code: Greatness Isn't Born. It's Grown. Here's How.* New York: Bantam Books, 2009.

CS Dweck, *Mindset: The New Psychology of Success.* New York: Random House, 2006.

K. Anders Ericsson, N Charness, PJ Feltovich & RR Hoffman, eds., *The Cambridge Handbook of Expertise and Expert Performance.* New York: Cambridge University Press, 2006.

M Gladwell, *Outliers: The Story of Success.* New York: Little Brown and Company, 2008.

JP Kotter & DS Cohen, *The Heart of Change: Real Life Stories of How People Change.* Boston: Harvard Business School Press, 2002.

JM Kouzes, BZ Posner, with E Biech, *A Coach's Guide to Developing Exemplary Leaders.* San Francisco: Jossey-Bass, 2010.

R Charan, S Drotter & J Noel, *The Leadership Pipeline: How to Build the Leadership Powered Company.* San Francisco: Jossey-Bass, 2001.

MK Schwartz, ed., *Leadership Resources: A Guide to Training and Development Tools* (8th edition). Greensboro, NC: Center for Creative Leadership, 2000.

N Tichy with E Cohen, *The Leadership Engine: How Winning Companies Build Leaders at Every Level.* New York: HarperCollins, 1997.

Index

More on *The Leadership Challenge...*

If you are looking for opportunities to make a difference in your world or tools to keep your community inspired, we can help. Whether you would like to read more works by Jim Kouzes and Barry Posner, gather feedback on your own leadership style, or implement a leadership development program within your organisation, we offer abundant resources for *The Leadership Challenge* (TLC) to help you begin or continue your leadership journey. These include:

- **Books** — Jim and Barry's best-selling, award-winning books include *The Leadership Challenge, The Truth About Leadership, Credibility, A Leaders' Legacy, Encouraging the Heart, The Student Leadership Challenge, The Academic Administrator's Guide to Exemplary Leadership* and *Making Extraordinary Things Happen in Asia.*
- **Workbooks** — *The Leadership Challenge Workbook, The Encouraging the Heart Workbook*, and *Strengthening Credibility* help you put TLC's teachings into practice. These interactive tools are designed to apply Jim and Barry's framework to productively resolving the problems and situations you face.
- **Assessments** — The Leadership Practices Inventory® (LPI®) — is the 360-degree assessment instrument designed by Jim and Barry that has recorded responses from over three million individuals worldwide. Find out more at www.lpionline.com. The Student LPI is also available for high school and undergraduate students.

In addition, The Encouragement Index can also help strengthen and develop your competence in the leadership practice of Encouraging the Heart.

- **Digital Offerings** — *The Leadership Challenge* DVD (3rd edition) is an approximately 90-minute film in which Jim and Barry introduce The Five Practices of Exemplary Leadership® to viewers through commentary and case studies. It includes a guide for screening and discussion, *The Leadership Challenge* eLearning Program is a two-hour self-paced course intended to build awareness around the model. It is an excellent introduction to Jim and Barry's work and has many appplications, such as pre-work for assessment administration or as a way to cascade the model through an organisation. *The Leadership Challenge* Mobile App helps individuals integrate the leadership practices presented in this book into their lives and daily routines. It includes content from the book and on The Five Practices, as well as features and functionality to help users make plans, take action on recommended activities and obtain feedback. You can download the Mobile App from the iTunes store.

- **Workshops** — *The Leadership Challenge*® Workshop is a unique, intensive program that has served as a catalyst for profound leadership transformations in organisations of all sizes and in all industries. In this highly interactive workshop, participants experience and apply Jim and Barry's leadership model through video cases, workbook exercises, group problem-solving tasks, lectures and outdoor action learning. For those looking to follow up a workshop experience with a deep-dive into the fifth practice, the Encouraging the Heart Workshop is an excellent solution. The Challenge Continues offers in-person and virtual solutions to refresh leaders on the model and provides opportunities to put the learning into practice.

These offerings represent the authoritative breadth and broad applicability of the ideas that make Jim and Barry the most trusted sources on becoming a better leader. To find out more about these products, and others by the authors, please visit www.leadershipchallenge.com. If you would like to speak to a leadership consultant about bringing *The Leadership Challenge* to your organisation or team, email leadership@wiley.com.

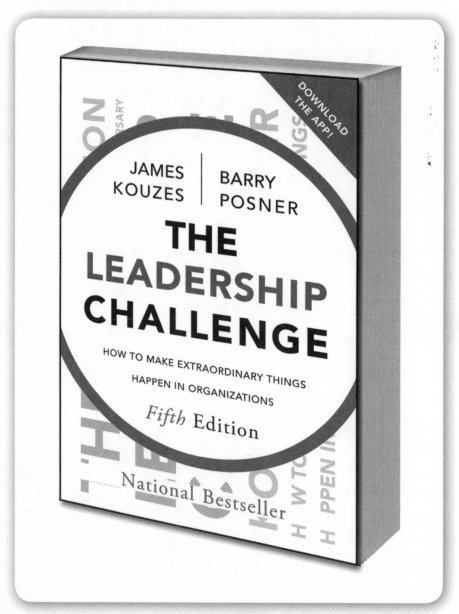